INDIAN
ALPHABET

CALLIGRAPHIC HISTORY AND
MYSTIC FUNCTION OF THE
BRAHMI WRITING SYSTEM

Written and Illustrated by

M B Jackson

GREEN MAGIC

Green Magic
53 Brooks Road
Street
Somerset BA16 0PP
England

info@greenmagicpublishing.com
www.greenmagicpublishing.com

ISBN 9780995547834

Designed and typeset by
K.DESIGN, Winscombe, Somerset

GREEN MAGIC

"*To copy the alphabet is an act of worship, the letters themselves are objects of contemplation. Meditation on them should culminate in the grand vision of the 'Garland of Letters,' the embodiment of being, set in the sound and form of the alphabet.*"

Mahavairochana Sutra

Contents

Indian Alphabet

After Mesopotamia and Egypt, India is the worlds third oldest civilization. It has the world's second largest population, who speak more than 427 languages and over 1000 dialects derived from four major language groups, written in over fifty variant scripts. The adaptation of the Indian writing system to record the native tongues of southeast Asia makes the Indian alphabet the parent of the world's largest script family.

Writing began on the Indian subcontinent around 3200 BCE with the pictographic script of the Indus Valley civilization. Following its collapse around 2000 BCE, writing seems to have vanished from the continent with only a scant record of signs found. No direct link between the Indus pictographic script and the creation of the Brahmi script in 250 BCE has been established and its influence is hotly debated.

The irony about the extended Brahmi script family is that its existence may be due to the low status given to writing by the ancient Hindu priests called Vedic Brahmins, who spoke the refined Indo-Aryan dialect called Sanskrit. Originally received by Brahma from the Supreme Lord Krishna, the word Vedas means knowledge. Vedic Sanskrit has its own grammar and it is only used in the Vedas, no new book can be composed in Vedic Sanskrit. The words have accent, akin to musical notes and a words meaning can change drastically if the accent of its letters are changed.

In ancient India, Veda spread orally through word of mouth, from the master (Shruti – that which is remembered) to the disciple (Smurti – that which is heard). Therefore these words have to be heard from the Guru properly for the right accent. No one has the authority to change even a single syllable of the Smurti. They are passed from one age to the other by the sense of hearing, by the Gurus who then recite them to the disciples and the practice goes on. As Vedism was an oral religion, the Brahmins never created a writing system.

On the other hand, both the Jains and the Buddhists endorsed the importance of writing to propagate their scriptures. Buddha insisted his teachings be written in Prakrit, the vernacular or common form of Sanskrit. It may have been this revolutionary approach to religious conversion that made the extended Brahmi script family possible.

Scripts styles and languages

Following the institution of the Brahmi script in 250 BCE, it gradually evolved through the centuries via dynastic variants, before diversifying into localized variants during the middle ages, to blossom into the rich variety of modern calligraphic and typographic forms. In general, these scripts form two categories; northern – angular, square, used for writing Indo-Aryan; and southern – rounded, curved, used for writing Dravidian. There are also a number of mixed scripts such as Gurmukhi, Oriya and Sinhala, composed of angular and rounded forms used to write Indo-Aryan. These two categories can be extended to the national scripts of Nepal, Tibet and Mongolia which are northern Brahmi variants. While the national scripts of Burma, Thailand, Cambodia and Laos are southern Brahmi variants.

Indian influence

The influence of Indian religion and trade took the Brahmi writing system to many non Indian speaking countries. In southeast Asia, the Brahmi system was adapted to write the Pali Cannon of Orthodox or Theravada Buddhism in the local script. While Hindu, Shivite and Buddhist inscriptions inspired the creation of the native, pre Arabic and Roman scripts of Indonesia. In Central Asia, the Himalayas and the Orient, Hindu, Shivite, Mahayana and Vjrayana Buddhists texts were written in Sanskrit using Indian script styles, that over the centuries have achieved sacred status outside of India, helping to create the extended Brahmi script family. In Japan and Ethiopia, the Brahmi abugida was the inspiration behind the creation of the alpha-syllabic Kana and Amharic writing systems.

Conquest has also played a role in writing on the Indian sub-continent. Because so many languages, dialects and scripts were used across the country, there was no established common language or script. Both the conquering Muslims and British established the Arabic and English systems as the lingua franca of their empires. It wasn't until independence from Britain in 1947 that an Indian government established the Devanagari script as a national writing system, not only for writing standardised Sanskrit and Hindi but adapted to write other Indian languages and dialects.

Religion and Mysticism

India is the original home of four of the world's major religions. Hinduism is the modern word for Vedism or Brahmanism and includes Shivaism. The term was introduced in colonial days to distinguish it from Islam. Buddhism is no longer practiced in India. Jainism remains a minority religion. Sikhism is a mixture of Hindu and Islamic beliefs. Zoroastrianism, Judaism, Christianity and Islam arrived in India during the first millennium CE and have influenced the development of Hinduism.

In common with Western occult systems, the Indian alphabet represents Universal Creation through sound vibration as encoded in language, but cabala is not its prime magical function. The prime mystical function of the Indian alphabet is physical, mental and spiritual healing and expansion of consciousness through the use of seed sounds or bija (Om), combined with chanting, meditation, yoga, and psychoactive tools like mantras, yantras and mandalas.

Indian Alphabet

Brahmi	Gupta	Siddham	Devanagari	Bengali	Gujarati	Gurmukhi	Oriya	Ranjana	Uchen

Northern India - Nagari (headed script styles) Indo-Aryan

Pallava	Old Grantha	Grantha	Vatteluttu	Tamil	Telugu	Malayalam	Sinhala	Burmese	Khmer

Southern India - (rounded script styles) Dravidian

calligraphic variation in the Brahmi script family

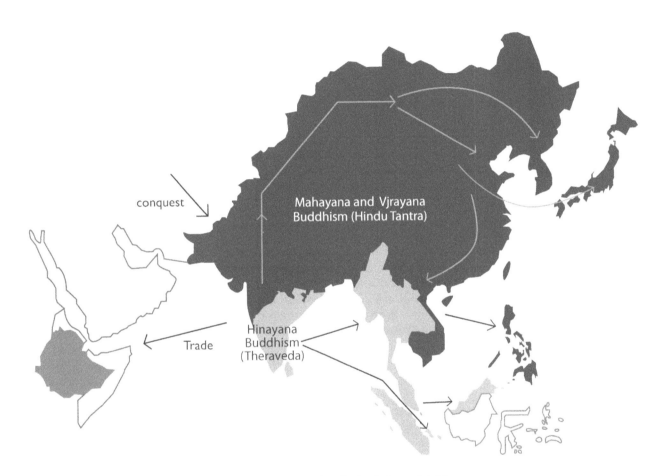

sphere of influence of India in Asia and Africa

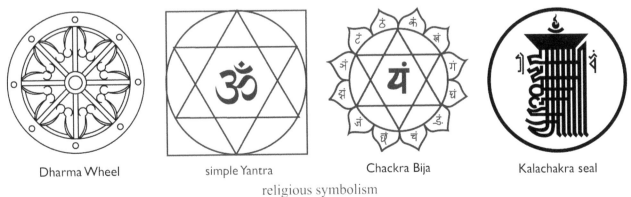

Dharma Wheel	simple Yantra	Chackra Bija	Kalachakra seal

religious symbolism

Religion

Religion has played the most important role in the development of the Indian alphabet, being the origin of its creation and its dispersal. India is the birthplace of four of the worlds major religions, Hinduism, Buddhism, Jainism and Sikhism. The origin of three of these religions can be found in the Vedic religion of the migrating Aryan peoples who settled in the Indus valley, where earlier native Dravidian religious concepts and practises were centered in India's pre-history. The influence of Dravidian religious and cultural practises on the Aryan Vedic religion are disputed. But the worship of Shiva, the fertility orientated mother goddess and village deities are recognized as a survivor of the pre-Vedic, Dravidian religion in southern India, Tamil Nadu and Sri Lanka, where these practises are strongest.

Vedism, also called Brahmanism led to spiritual and moral differences causing Buddhists and Jains to breakaway from Vedic-Brahmanism during the 6th century BCE. Later in history, early Christianity is thought to have had a major influence on Indian religious beliefs, giving it the concept of the Trinity and idol worship in the form of statue making, which were absent throughout the pre-Christian era. During the medieval and renaissance periods, conflict between Hinduism and Islam led to the creation of Sikhism, a reconciliation of both philosophies.

Hinduism

The modern religion known as Hinduism was first given its name in the 13th century to distinguish it from Islam. It is seen as a religion based on mythology, it has no founder unlike Buddhism, Christianity and Confucianism, and no fixed cannon such as the Bible, Qur'an or Tipitaka. It contains a myriad of local cults and traditions which all share the common belief of Karma – the chain of cause and effect in the world of morality. It inspired the breakaway, unorthodox religions of Jainism and Buddhism, who do not recognise the Hindu sacred texts or Vedas but retain core concepts such as karma.

The Vedas are a collection of hymns venerated by the ritualistic Brahmins, a priestly caste who practised the oral tradition of the Rig Veda, or knowledge, speaking a sacred language called Sanskrit. Their emphasis on correct pronunciation of Sanskrit influenced the Vjrayana school or Diamond Vehicle of esoteric Hindus and later Tantric Buddhists to believe the universe is created from sound, and that spoken language is a resonance of a primaeval seed or root language called Bija, the sonic energies of Creation or Gods. Because the Hindu religion believed sound to be spiritual perfection, their theology was always transmitted orally and wasn't canonized until 100 AD in Sri Lanka.

Buddhism

The historical development of Buddhism begins in the 6th century BCE when its teachings were expounded by the Buddha and diffused by his disciples. The historical Buddha, Siddhartha Gautama Buddha, was the son of a prince, whose small kingdom was in the foothills of the Himalayas, in the modern state of Bihar. The Buddhist Sutras are said to have come straight from the mouth of Buddha who spoke Magdhi Prakrit, also called Pali. Their Holy book, the Pali Cannon or Tipitaka is regarded as the most authentic version of Buddha's word, the oldest form of Sutras as venerated by the Theravedic school of Hinayana Buddhism or the Elders school of the Little Vehicle.

The Sanskrit texts of the unorthodox Bodhisattvas school of Mahayana Buddhism or Great Vehicle, passed into Vietnam, China and Korea before the end of the 1st century CE. Japan by the 2nd century, Tibet and Mongolia by the 7th century. From the end of the 7th century onwards, Mahayana Buddhism was almost submerged by Vjrayana Buddhism or Tantric Hinduism, the Diamond Vehicle, which established itself in Tibet, Mongolia, China and Japan as Tantric Buddhism. Between the 10th and 13th centuries, Buddhism became mixed with Taoist and Confucian beliefs in China to form Ch'an or Zen Buddhism as it is called in Japan. After the 12th century, Buddhism became practically extinct in India, the country of its origin.

Jainism

Scarcely practiced outside India, Jainism is divided between two sects, the Svetambara or white robed, and Digmabara or sky robed meaning naked, and has around five million followers. According to the Jain doctrine, first pronounced by Vardhaman Mahavira, the cosmos functions through constant interaction between living creatures and five categories of inanimate objects, and that minerals, air, wind and fire, as well as plants possess souls with varying degrees of consciousness. Jains practice ahimsa, or the non-hurting of any life form. Jains believe that souls remain conscious of their identity through successive reincarnation, which is determined by the cumulative effect of conduct or karma. Since Jains believe that God is only the noblest and fullest manifestation of powers latent in the human soul, they can be described as agnostic.

Sikhism

Sikhism is a religion founded by Guru Nanak (1469-1538), an attempt to synthesise Hinduism and those of the invading Muslims into one formal belief system. They emphasise that both Allah and Brahman are pleased by surrender to God and the loving service of one's fellow human beings. Caste distinctions are not recognized. Sikhs believe in evolution, the law of karma and reincarnation. Liberation or union with God is made possible by one's personal efforts.

Religion

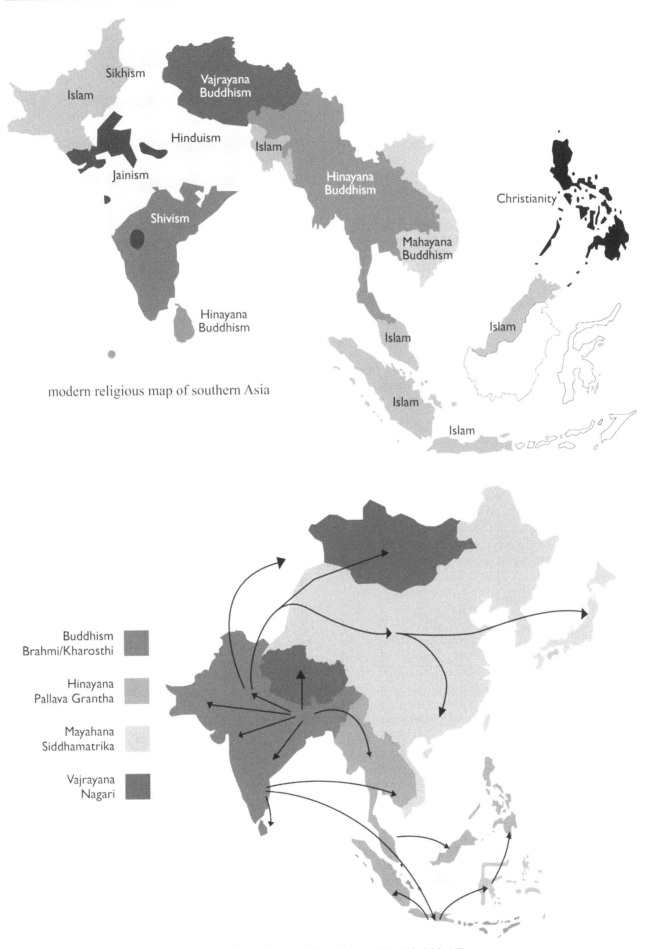

modern religious map of southern Asia

Buddhism
Brahmi/Kharosthi

Hinayana
Pallava Grantha

Mayahana
Siddhamatrika

Vajrayana
Nagari

scripts dispersion and Buddhism 250 BC-800 AD

Gods of Writing

To understand the relationship between the different Indian Gods of writing, a little knowledge of the metaphysical structure of the Trimurti and its relationship to OM, its partnership with Shakti or female energy and the cult of Tantra, the science of the Divine Word, is required. Indian cosmology is portrayed by a large pantheon of gods and goddess. These deities exist as married couples who represent the individual aspects of the Supreme Consciousness or Brahman, who brought about creation by chanting the mantra OM, from which all 51 sound vibrations of Vedic Sanskrit are derived.

The supreme consciousness is known as Brahman, and from this sphere is born the living cosmos. The cosmos evolves through three stages, creation, preservation and destruction. In the Hindu pantheon, these three aspects are represented by Brahma, Vishnu and Shiva, respectively. Together in their capacity as universal life itself, they are called the Trimurti. This triple aspect of creation is also symbolized in the supreme bija-mantra OM, in which the three individual sounds A U M correspond to the three stages and gods of the Trimurti, respectively.

The mystical knowledge contained within the Brahmi abugida is found in various Indian philosophies. The most popular in the West being Tantra, meaning to 'expand' (ones consciousness.) To achieve Tantra, the adept uses the meditative methods such as yoga, mantra and yantra to merge the individual self in to the universal self. In Tantra, the universal self is represented by the God Shiva, the founder or Primordial teacher of Tantra. The origins of Tantric practises can be traced back to the pre-Aryan, Indus civilization, where it originated in Shakti, worship of the power or energy of the Mother Goddess, which is closely associated with the pre-Aryan God, Shiva, giving Tantra great antiquity.

Brahma and Sarasvati

Brahma, the first god of the Trimurti, the Deva of Creation, not to be confused with Brahman, the Supreme Cosmic Spirit. Brahma is the creator of the universe, and all living things are said to have evolved from him. He is seen as a god of the intellect and of the mind, the source of all knowledge in the universe, credited as the inventor of all the arts of civilization: music, letters, mathematics and calendars. He inscribed the Vedic texts in Sanskrit on leaves of gold. While Brahma is a deity of equal importance to Shiva and Vishnu, he is not nearly as widely worshipped as the other two. The simple fact is, that since the universe has already been created, Brahma's work is done – for the time being.

Brahma's female consort is Sarasvati, goddess of eloquence, inventor of the Sanskrit language, music and poetry. As the Goddess Vak, she is the voice, the representation of the spoken word. The name Sarasvati comes from saras (meaning "flow") and wati (meaning "she who has ..."), i.e., "she who has flow". So, Saraswati is symbol of knowledge; its flow (or growth) is like a river, and knowledge is supremely alluring, like a beautiful woman. A tributary of the mighty Indus river was named

after her, also a alternative name for the Indus valley script and the meaning of the name of the Sarada script. Sarada being an alternative name for Sarasvatti and Saradadesh being an archaic name for Kashmir.

Ganesha the Scribe

The second God of the Trimuti is Vishnu, the preserver. His link to the Gods of Writing is through his son Ganesha, by his wife Parvati. Ganesha is one of the best-known and most-widely worshipped deities in the Hindu pantheon. His elephant-headed image is also venerated by Jains, Buddhists and beyond India. Known as the Remover of Obstacles and more generally as Lord of Beginnings, he is the patron of the arts and science, and the deva of intellect and wisdom. He is invoked as Patron of Letters during writing sessions.

Several texts relate mythological anecdotes to explain his distinct iconography. As a God of Writing they relate to his broken tusk. In the first part of the epic poem Mahabharata, the sage Vyasa asks Ganesha to transcribe the poem as he dictated it to him. The dictation began but in the rush of writing Ganesha broke his feather pen. He broke off a tusk and used it as a pen so that the transcription could proceed without interruption.

Shiva and Kali

Shiva is the deva responsible for the destruction of the universe. However, in Hindu mythology, creation always follows destruction – therefore Shiva is also associated with a reproductive force, restoring what was destroyed. Most Shivites (worshippers of Shiva) agree that in his highest form, Para Shiva, Shiva is both male and female at once – containing both the male Shiva and his female counterpart, the goddess, Shakti.

As this destroyer-reproductive force, Shiva is the Nataraja, the "Lord of the Cosmic Dance." He is the creator of dance, rhythm, and music. He is also said to have spoken or beaten out on a drum, the first sixteen rhythmic syllables ever pronounced, which formed the basis of the Sanskrit language.

Shiva's female consort is the goddess Kali (a fearsome goddess of destruction) on whose body she is often seen standing, suggesting that without the power of Kali or Shakti, Shiva or masculine energy is inert. Kali is the foremost of the Mahavidyas, ten ferocious tantric goddesses, Matrikas, who fought the demon, Rutabija on behalf of Shiva.

In her iconography, Kali wears the necklace of severed human heads which is variously enumerated. Containing 108, an auspicious number in Hinduism, the number of countable beads on a Japamala or rosary for repeating mantras. 50. 51 and 52 beads represent the sounds of Vedic Sanskrit in the form of the Varnamala of Bija or Garland of Letters, with which Kali destroys, re-creates and preserves the universe. Hindus believe that Sanskrit is the dynamic language of the Goddess, each letter represents a feminine energy (Shakti), a form of Kali. Therefore she is seen as the mother of all language, of all bija, mantra and shashtra.

Gods of Writing

Brahma
God of creation
first god of the Trimurti

Sarasvatti
Goddess of eloquence, poetry, music
consort of Brahma

Ganesha
God of Wisdom, Learning and Business
son of Vishnu and Parvati

Kali
Goddess of death, destruction and rebirth
consort of Shiva

Sanskrit

Sanskrit is a pre-eminent Indo-Ayran language spoken on the Indian sub-continent for over three and a half millennia. It is the liturgical language of Hinduism,Mahayana and Vjrayana Buddhism, the classic literary language of India and one of its 22 official tongues. It has a similar role to that of Latin in Europe, a language of learning that continues to be widely studied. Archeological evidence suggests Sanskrit was not a written language until the 2nd century CE, although the Brahmi writing system had been in existence in India for some five hundred years previous, although texts on Sanskrit grammar may have been in existence since 600 BCE.

The original form of Sanskrit was Vedic Sanskrit, that had become archaic by 600 BCE, when the language was re-invented as Classical Sanskrit. But neither language was written down at this time. In 250 BCE, the Brahmi script was developed to write Prakrit – common or vernacular Sanskrit. When Sanskrit became a written language, local variants of the Brahmi script were used to record it. Because of this, Sanskrit had no official script until Indian independence in the 1950s when the Devanagari script was chosen because of its historical association with Sanskrit texts.

Asia has many language groups that use scripts derived from the Indian writing system. Austro-Asian is the indigenous language group of south Asia, spoken across greater India and southeast Asia. Since prehistoric times, this has been enriched by various incoming language groups including Dravidian, Indo-Aryan and Tibeto-Burman. Later migrations introduced the Islamic, Perso-Arabic language and script, and colonial Christian languages such as Dutch, Portugese and English, written with Roman letters. The continent is also home to some isolated, natural languages such as Nihali and Burushaski that show no genealogical relationship with other languages.

Dravidian

Dravidian is a close knit language group thought to be indigenous to India, spoken by a racially mixed people who arrived there between the 4th and 3rd millennia BCE, replacing the prehistoric, indigenous Austro-Asian languages. The lingua franca of greater India, spoken before the arrival of Aryan tribes, around 1600 BCE. Following this date, Dravidian split into north, central and southern ancestral languages that remain independent of Sanskrit. Modern Dravidian has 75 languages with over 220 million speakers across southern India, Sri Lanka, Pakistan and Afghanistan. The major Dravidian languages are Tamil, Kannada, Malayalam, Telugu and Tulu. Although Malayalam and Telugu are originally Dravidian, over 80% of their lexicon is borrowed from Sanskrit.

Sanskrit

Sanskrit is the mother tongue of most North Indian languages. Aryan speaking tribes crossed from Afghanistan and Iran into northwest India around 1600 BCE, colonizing the whole of northern and central India. They spoke the Old Indic language which their priests refined into a divine dialect called Sanskrit, (Samaskrta – perfected, cultivated), the language of priests, the intellectual elite, official proclamations, Vedic ritual and commentaries. Its evolution is classified into Old Indo-Aryan (Vedic) 1500-600 BCE, Middle Indo-Aryan (classic) 600 BCE-1000 CE, New Indo-Aryan (medieval) 1000-1300 CE, and Modern 1300 – present.

Sanskrit as spoken in the Vedas, prevailed until around 600 BC when it assumed its classical form, an evolution hastened by the efforts of early scholars to standardize grammar. In the early 5th century BCE, Yaska's Nirutka explained Vedic words that were already obsolete, and Panini's Ashtadhayayi extrapolated 4000 rules for spoken Sanskrit.

In order to maintain the purity of the Vedas – transmitted orally from generation to generation by highly trained memorizers – it became necessary to develop phonetics. This led to a Sanskrit alphabet, which began with vowels and progressed to consonants, grouped together according to the manner in which they were read aloud through the use of the tongue, lips, teeth and throat. While this alphabet was easy to master, the inflection driven Sanskrit was not. Depending on its inflection, a single word denotes, person, gender, number, tense, case, and word compounding is common. Unable to master these complexities, common folk made less and less use of Sanskrit, and replaced inflections with prepositions to create Prakrit, vernacular or common speech.

Prakrit

After 600 BCE different tongues began to develop from classical Sanskrit. Common people found the sounds and grammar much too difficult. They took to speaking a simpler version of Sanskrit called Prakrit – normal, vernacular, which had several dialects. Modern Indo-Aryan languages are derived from these Prakrits – Hindi, Assamese, Bengali, Gujarati, Marathi, Punjabi, Rajasthani, Oriya and Sinhala, evolved into distinct recognizable languages during the medieval or New Indo-Aryan age.

The Brahmi script was originally devised to write Prakrit. Ardhamagdhi Prakrit, is considered to be the definitive form of Prakrit, originally used to write the Jain scriptures, other Prakrits are considered variants of it. The literary Prakrits of Ardhramagdhi, Magdhi and Pali are synonymous with each other on similar points. The oldest preserve historical forms and many different noun inflections in many metrical places. Buddha spoke Magdhi Prakrit and his teaching were written in Magdhi, later known as Pali, as well as in Sanskrit. Because of this Magdhi or Pali Prakrit became the liturgical language of Theravada Buddhism, written in the regional variant of the Brahmi script.

Sanskrit

Northwest - Indo-Aryan
Pakistan (Baluchistan
North West Frontier
Northern Areas,
Punjab, Sindh, Telengana) - *Urdu*
Jammu & Kashmir - *Kashmiri*
Punjab - *Punjabi, Dogri*
Nepal - *Nepali*

North/Central - Indo-Aryan
Uttar Pradesh, Bihar,
Himachal Pradesh, Haryana,
Rajasthan, Uttar Pradesh,
Madhya Pradesh, Chhatisgarh,
Jharkhand, Bihar, Sikkim - *Hindi/Hindustani*
Gujarat - *Gujarati*
Maharastra, Madhya Pradesh - *Marathi*

South - Indo-Aryan
Sri Lanka - *Sinhala*
Maldives - *Maldivian*

South - Dravidian
Madhya Pradesh - *Gondi*
Andhra Pradesh - *Telugu*
Goa, Karnataka - *Kannada*
Karnataka, Kerala - *Tulu*
Kerala - *Malayalam*
Tamil Nadu - *Tamil*

Northeast - Indo-Aryan
Bihar - *Bhojpuri, Magahi, Maithili*
Assam - *Assamese*
West Bengal, Bangladesh - *Bengali*
Orissa - *Oriya*

Northwest - Tibeto-Burman
Arunachal Pradesh - *Thanyi*
1. Nagaland - *Ao*
2. Manipur- *Manipuri*
3. Mizoram - *Mizo*
4. Tripura - *Konkani*
5. Meghalaya - *Khasi & Garo*

Greater Indian language map

अ आ इ ई उ ऊ ऋ ॠ ल लृ ए ऐ ओ औ आं अँ आः
a aa i ii u uu ri rii lri lrii e ai o au am an ah

क ख ग घ ङ च छ ज झ ट ठ ड ढ ण
ka kha ga gha nga ca cha ja jha tta ttha dda ddha nna

त थ द ध न प फ ब भ म य र ल व श ष स ह क्ष
ta tha da dha na pa pha ba bha ma ya ra la va sha ssha sa ha ksha

Vedic Sanskrit

अ आ इ ई उ ऋ ए ओ
a aa i ii u r e o

क ख ग घ ङ च छ ज झ अ
ka kha ga gha nga ca cha ja jha nya

ट ठ ड ढ ण त थ द ध न
tta ttha dda ddha nna ta tha da dha na

प फ ब भ म य र ल व श ष स ह ळ
pa pha ba bha ma ya ra la va sha ssha sa ha lla

Pali Prakrit

Brahmi Abugida

Brahmi abugida is a western academic term used to describe the Indian alphabet, called Varnamala or Aksaramala in India. Named Brahmi after the priests who invented it, and abugida to dentote its alphasylabic function. It is the parent of the worlds largest script family and the inspiration behind the creation of two international writing systems, Japanese Kana and Ethiopian Amharic.

The system was first developed around 250 BCE, to write the Sanskrit dialect of Magdhi Prakrit, also called Pali. It was later extended to write Vedic Sanskrit. The number of letters it contains varies on which language it is being used to write. Vedic Sanskrit requires 50, 51 or 52 letters with Classical Sanskrit requiring only 46. Prakrits like Hindi require 44, while Pali requires only 42. At its most elaborate, it is composed of 52 letters, employing 16 vowels, 11 of which are in frequent use – a, aa, u, uu, i, ii, ri, e, ai, o, au. Its 33 to 36 consonant-syllables are arranged in a logical scheme according to the order of speech organs involved, throat, palette, the teeth and lips. Allowing them to be divided into two sets and eight groups called vargas, which are subdivided into categories called ganas.

It employs four forms of phoneme or letter. Independent vowels called svara and modifying vowels called matra. Consonant-syllables called vyanjana, and conjunct consonants called samyukt. The vowel-consonants 'am' and 'ah' are signified by ayogavahah, special diacritic marks.

All the letters are capital forms, written from left to right. In northern India, the script is characterized by the horizontal bar called Shro Rekha, from which each letter hangs. In southern Indian, it is characterized by being rounded. These calligraphic distinctions are the result of employing different writing materials. Following Indian independence in the 1950s, Devanagari was chosen as its official script, for its strong religious and cultural associations, although Sanskrit can be written in anyone of the many Brahmi derived scripts.

There are four basic forms of punctuation; the dash or horizontal bar; the vertical bar; dot; circle. Sentences are marked at the end by a perpendicular stroke called Viram, two such strokes are used at the end of a text. Word boundaries are not marked, as the horizontal top bars are usually linked to form an unbroken line. The line is only broken between words with a final vowel, diphthong, nasal (anusvara) or weak aspirant (visarga) and words with an initial consonant. Rather than writing a succession of individual words, Sanskrit orthography is sensitive to breath groups representing connected discourse.

Spelling has been eliminated in Sanskrit because every sound has been correctly analyzed and placed into its phonetic classification and the consonants and the vowels which have different functions, have been assigned definite modes of behavior. Whereas, the combinations of letters used in Roman script for sounds which have no signs, created the need for spelling them artificially necessary.

Vowels (svara and matra)

The Brahami abugida employs two forms of vowel, independent vowels called svara, and modifying vowels called matra. Each vowel is realizable in three scales, short, long, prolonged. All vowels can be pronounced in non-nasal and nasal modes, which means each vowel can be pronounced 18 different ways based on timing, manner and accent of pronunciation. Since it is not possible to record these differences, they must be remembered by listening.

As pronunciation was to be very accurately managed, the Indian grammarians made differentiation between the signs for the short and long sounds of the same vowel. It will be seen that the vowels which are short, flourish to the left and their longer signs to the right. This is noticeable in Devanagari, Tamil, Malayalam and other scripts of the South Indians who were very careful in preserving their traditions.

Altogether there are 16 vowels, seven independent vowels, a, i, u, ri, li, e, o, each having two forms, aa, ii, uu, rii, lii, ai, au, making fourteen altogether. The initial or independent vowel form is used alone, at the beginning of words or after another vowel. It is also used when there is no consonant for the vowel to attach to. Out of these fourteen vowels, thirteen come in two forms, initial or independent (svara), and dependant, medial or modifying (matra). There is no modifying form for the short 'a' because this vowel sound is the inherent vowel sound of all unmodified consonant sounds. The addition of the two vowel-consonants, aM and aH, bring the total to 16.

Matra is the Sanskrit term for what Westerners call dependent, medial or modifying vowels. In Sanskrit, all syllables are consonants with an inherent vowel 'a', as in 'ka, ga, ta,'. The sound of this vowel can be changed by adding a modifying vowel sign to the consonant letter, in a similar fashion to that of diacritic marks. They are used to neutralise the inherent 'a' sound in order to indicate either, that another vowel is attached to the consonant or to change the sound of the vowel, ka, ki, ko. kai, kee. Matra not only refers to the sign of the dependent vowel but also the new letter shape created when attached to a consonant. They are always depicted in combination with a single consonant or a consonant cluster.

Consonants (vyanjana and samyukt)

A vowel attached to a consonant is called a syllable. In the Brahmi writing system a syllable is an effective orthographic unit formed from a consonant with an inherent vowel 'a' sound, as in 'ka', ga', 'ta', etc. Their Indian name is Vyanjana. The first set of 25 consonants are called occlusive, the remainder are called non-occlusive. The occlusive group are divided into five vargas or groups based on gutturals, palatals, cerebrals or retroflex, dentals and labials. The eight non-occlusive consonants are divided in to three vargas, semi-vowels, sibilants (anasthas) and aspirates (uusman), each having four, three and one letter respectively, are treated separately.

Brahmi Abugida

अ आ इ ई उ ऊ ऋ ॠ ल ए ऐ ओ औ आं आः

ा ि ी ु ू ृ ॄ ॢ े ै ो ौ ं ः

| a | aa | i | ii | u | uu | ri | rii | li | e | ai | o | au | am | ah |

top - initial vowels (svara)   bottom - medial vowels (matra)

प पा पि पी पु पू पृ पॄ पॢ पे पै पो पौ पां पाः

| pa | paa | pi | pii | pu | puu | pri | prii | pli | pe | pai | po | pau | pam | pah |

diacritic vowel placement (matra)

vowels (svara and matra)

group/catagory varga/gana	mute-consonants sparsa				nasals anunasika	semi-vowels antahstha	sibliants usman
	-V-A	-V+A	+V-A	+V+A	+V	+V	-V
gutterals kanthya	क ka	ख kha	ग ga	घ gha	ङ nga		ह ha
palatals talavya	च ca	छ cha	ज ja	झ jha	ञ nya	य ya	श sa
cerebals (retroflex) murdhanya	ट tta	ठ ttha	ड dda	ढ ddha	ण nna	र ra	ष ssha
dentals dantya	त ta	थ tha	द da	ध dha	न na	ल la	स sha
labials osthya	प pa	फ pha	ब ba	भ bha	म ma	व va	

-V non-voiced; -A non-aspirate; +V voiced; +A aspirate

Consonants (vyanjana)

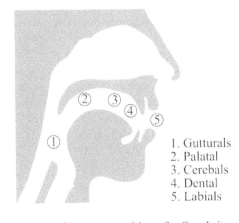

1. Gutturals
2. Palatal
3. Cerebals
4. Dental
5. Labials

tongue placement positions for Sanskrit

क्ष ज्ञ त्र ज्ञ श्र ह्म त्क ड्ड

| ksha | jna | tra | jna | sra | hma | ttka | dhdha |

conjunct consonants / ligatures (samyukt)

पृ ़प अं अः अँ

| virana | halanta | anusvara (m) | visarga (h) | chandrabindu |

diacritic marks (ayogavaha)

क़ ख़ ग़ ज़ झ़ फ़ ड़ ढ़

| qa | h | ga | za | zha | fa | ra | rha |

additional consonants for loan words

Brahmi Abugida

The system distinguishes between cerebral or retroflex sounds (tta, ttha, dda, ddha, na), and dental sounds (ta, tha, da, dha, na). The difference is subtle and does not occur in English, in which almost all consonants are partial aspirated. Producing the cerebral or retroflex sounds involves curling the tip of the tongue against the palette and then releasing it. Dental sounds involve placing the tip of the tongue against the upper part of the top teeth. These two groups are usually distinguished by the inclusion of a double intial letter or by placing a dot under the initial consonant of the cerebal forms.

Vargas and ganas are phonetic sequences. Vargas are based on the position of the speech organs when pronouncing the sound. Ganas denote the phonetic sequencing of voiced and unvoiced sounds. Each varga is identified by its initial letters – ka, ca, tta, ta, pa, ya, sa, ha. Hence, the varga that contains the phonetic sequence – ka, kha, ga, gha, na is referred to as the ka-varga. The phonetic sequence – ca, cha, ja, jna, na, form the ca – varga and so on. They are based on how the sounds are produced by different parts of the mouth, lips, teeth, cheeks, etc., when the tongue touches the part of the lobe above the tongue.

The first five vargas, ka, ca, tt, ta, pa, are futher divided into two categories, plosive and voiced plosives. 'Na' the last consonant in the varga is the nasal consonant. The plosive and the voiced plosive are again divided into unaspirated and aspirated. These form four phonetic sequences of six letters that finish with a semi-vowel, all of which are referred to as ganas. The phonetic sequence that forms the ganas begin with the initial consonants, ka, kha, ga, gha, and end with the semi-vowels ya, ra, va, la.

Conjuncts or ligatures called Samyukt are a combination of two to five consonants. There are about 1000 conjuncts in the Brahmi abugida. Some partly retain the shape of the constituent consonant, while others are not clearly derived from the letters making up their components. They are formed by adding a distinctive stroke only to the letter which keeps its inherent vowel. For example the consonant cluster 'nta' is represented by conjoining the letters for 'na' and 'ta' to form the conjunct consonant 'nta'.

Diacritc marks (ayogavahah)

Ayogavahah are special diacritic glyphs employed to change the sound of a letter. They modifify a letter by being placed above, below, before or after a letter. Consonants can have their inherent vowel muted by a Virana, an oblique stroke added to the bottom of the downstroke of a consonant letter, or by a Halanta, a small dot placed below a letter. Jihvamuliya and Upadhmaniya use the semi-visarga pronounced before the letter. Weak aspiration is represented by the Visarga, a dot placed above a letter. The nasal Anusvara, a vowel sound is marked by a colon placed after the letter. The Anunasika or Chandrada is a half-moon mark placed over a letter indicating nasalization. Chandrabindhu is a halfmoon topped with a dot. There is also another set of consonants added for the transliteration of loan words from Persian, Arabic and English, marked by a special diacritic mark called a Nukta, a dot placed at the bottom left of a letter.

Brahmi Derived Systems

Over the centuries, through religion and trade, the Brahmi abugida has been the inspiration for the creation of two major writing systems. In the Far East, thanks to the spread of Buddhism, the Japanese took the idea of a syllabic alphabet to write the Altiac language called Nipponese, and applied it to their abstracted Chinese character script to create the Kana writing system. Trade between India and Africa led to the creation of the Amharic syllabary to write Ethiopian. Merchants and traders already used a variant of the Semitic abjad, a consonant only alphabet, and under Indian influence the script became alpha-syllabic.

Kana

The Japanese simplified Kanji or Chinese characters to produce Kana, a general term used to describe various syllabic writing systems they created. Kana 'non-regular writing' signs are used as reading aids in annoting Buddhist texts. Because of this Buddhist influence there are also traces of an Indian influence.

The two Kana systems used in modern Japanese are Hiragana and Katakana. They have 48 characters each, 5 representing independent vowels, the rest syllables of the consonant/vowel type called mora, or short syllable. Two diacritics are employed, dakuten or nigoriten, two little strokes, and handakuten, a small circle. Both scripts can be written in columns from top to bottom, and in horizontal lines from left to right.

Amharic

Amharic is a Semitic language written in the Brahmi influenced, Ethiopic alpha-syllabic, Amharic script. Around 500 BC, the South Semitic script evolved to write the Semitic languages of Southern Arabia. Arabian settles took the South Semitic derived Sabaic script to Ethiopia, where, as the Ge'ez language, it evolved into Old Ethiopic, the language of the Ethiopic church. From the 4th century AD, under Indian influence, the script became alpha-syllabic, it became written from left to right and included vowel indication. This remodelled script became Classic Ethiopian from which the modern Amharic script was adapted in the 15th century AD.

Japanese Kana

Hiragana

a あ	i い	u う	e え	o お
ka か	ki き	ku く	ke け	ko こ
sa さ	si し	su す	se せ	so そ
ta た	ti ち	tu つ	te て	to と
na な	ni に	nu ぬ	ne ね	no の
ha は	hi ひ	hu ふ	he へ	ho ほ
ma ま	mi み	mu む	me め	mo も
ya や		yu ゆ		yo よ
ra ら	ri り	ru る	re れ	ro ろ
wa わ	wi ゐ		we ゑ	wo を
				n ん

Katakana

a ア	i イ	u ウ	e エ	o オ
ka カ	ki キ	ku ク	ke ケ	ko コ
sa サ	si シ	su ス	se セ	so ソ
ta タ	ti チ	tu ツ	te テ	to ト
na ナ	ni ニ	nu ヌ	ne ネ	no ノ
ha ハ	hi ヒ	hu フ	he ヘ	ho ホ
ma マ	mi ミ	mu ム	me メ	mo モ
ya ヤ		yu ユ		yo ヨ
ra ラ	ri リ	ru ル	re レ	ro ロ
wa ワ	wi ヰ		we ヱ	wo ヲ
n ン				

Amharic / Ethiopian

	a	u	i	a	e	e	o
p	ሀ	ሁ	ሂ	ሃ	ሄ	ህ	ሆ
f	ለ	ሉ	ሊ	ላ	ሌ	ል	ሎ
d	ሐ	ሑ	ሒ	ሓ	ሔ	ሕ	ሖ
s	መ	ሙ	ሚ	ማ	ሜ	ም	ሞ
P	ሠ	ሡ	ሢ	ሣ	ሤ	ሥ	ሦ
t	ረ	ሩ	ሪ	ራ	ሬ	ር	ሮ
g	ሰ	ሱ	ሲ	ሳ	ሴ	ስ	ሶ
d	ቀ	ቁ	ቂ	ቃ	ቄ	ቅ	ቆ
j	በ	ቡ	ቢ	ባ	ቤ	ብ	ቦ
z	ተ	ቱ	ቲ	ታ	ቴ	ት	ቶ
'(o)	ኀ	ኁ	ኂ	ኃ	ኄ	ኅ	ኆ
w	ነ	ኑ	ኒ	ና	ኔ	ን	ኖ
k	አ	ኡ	ኢ	ኣ	ኤ	እ	ኦ
'(a)	ከ	ኩ	ኪ	ካ	ኬ	ክ	ኮ
n	ወ	ዉ	ዊ	ዋ	ዌ	ው	ዎ
h	ዐ	ዑ	ዒ	ዓ	ዔ	ዕ	ዖ
t	ዘ	ዙ	ዚ	ዛ	ዜ	ዝ	ዞ
b	የ	ዩ	ዪ	ያ	ዬ	ይ	ዮ
q	ደ	ዱ	ዲ	ዳ	ዴ	ድ	ዶ
s	ገ	ጉ	ጊ	ጋ	ጌ	ግ	ጎ
r	ጠ	ጡ	ጢ	ጣ	ጤ	ጥ	ጦ
s	ጰ	ጱ	ጲ	ጳ	ጴ	ጵ	ጶ
m	ጸ	ጹ	ጺ	ጻ	ጼ	ጽ	ጾ
h	ፀ	ፁ	ፂ	ፃ	ፄ	ፅ	ፆ
l	ፈ	ፉ	ፊ	ፋ	ፌ	ፍ	ፎ
h	ፐ	ፑ	ፒ	ፓ	ፔ	ፕ	ፖ

offspring systems of the Brahmi abugida

Vendanga

In Hinduism, Vedanga means "limbs of the Vedas", they are six auxiliary disciplines developed in ancient times which perform various supportive and augmentary functions, an integral and essential part of the ancient Vedic education system. To a certain extent the vendangas were partly responsible for the popularity of Sanskrit as the main language of communication in ancient India.

They also played an influential role in the development of native languages (Prakrits, Dravidian, Tibeto-Burman), providing the basic framework on which they could grow. The vendangas came about because the language of the Vedic texts composed centuries earlier grew too archaic for the people of that time, around 600 BCE.

The six vendangas are; Shiksha – pronunciation, Chandra – meter, Vyakarana – grammar, Nirukta – linguistic analysis, Kalapa – standardization, Jyosha – time keeping. Quoted by the eminent scholar Yaska in the 5th century BCE, it is unknown when and where the list of six vendangas were conceived.

From around the 5th century BCE, Indian scholars devised memory aids in the form of poems and diagrams to explain certain aspects of Vendanga such as pronunciation and grammar. The science of Sanskrit was held in such high esteem it was thought worthy of worship, leading to certain educational memory aids acquiring sacred status. The vendagas were taught by other Indic religions which relied on Sanskrit for their education systems and religious practices. Because of the emergence of new methods of worship and temple traditions which took precedent over Vedic traditions in many parts of India, the vendangas have lost much of their influence.

Aksara Chakra

Underneath a mosque built in Dhara of Madhra Preadesh, lies a buried temple to Sarasvatti, Goddess of poetry and eloquence (speech). Discovered inside the temple was a wheel with verses and grammatic rules inscribed on it in the form of a chart. It is said that grammar can be learnt at a glance from this wheel. Because language is a science, it is worthy of worship, that is why the wheel inscribed with grammar was installed in the tomb. From this we learn that shastras like grammar were not regarded merely as of worldly interest, but in fact considered worthy or worship. The Aksara Chakra or Matrika Chakra, is a memory aid that explains how the Sanskrit 'A' as a root-vibration or bija, creates the other Sanskrit sounds and orders them.

Mashesvara Sutra (Shiva Sutra)

Between the 6th and 4th century BCE, the Indian scholar Panini formulated his treatise, the Ashtadhayayi or 'eight chapters.' It became the foundation text of Sanskrit grammar or Vyakarana. At the beginning of the text is the Mahesvara Sutra, more popularly called the Shiva Sutra. The sutra is a list of fourteen lines of verses that organise the phonemes of Sanskrit, vowels and consonants, arranged into clusters called Pratyahara which ends with a dummy sound called Anubandha, which refers to the last verse. Developed from Vedic Sanskrit it became the model for the pronunciation of Classical Sanskrit. The Meshasvara Sutra is just a collection of sounds. If you say them aloud, in one breath, they really sound like drumbeats. And because they came from a divine source, they were so perfect, so complete, that Panini was able to create, compile and codify the rules of Sanskrit grammar, in such a way as they have remained unchanged.

Varnanaga-kripanika

In the Ashtadhayayi, on the right side of where the Mashesvara Sutra ends, we find the beginning of the bandha know as the Varnanaga-kripanika, a metaphor mentioned in the 12th century, in Dhara, Madhrya Praedesh. It refers to Sanskrit language (syllables, pronunciation, morphology) depicted in a metaphor of dagger of Sanskrit rules. Varnanaga-kripanika is, as the expression indicates, a scimitar or dagger formed by the (combination) of the letters and a snake. The head of the snake is represented by the broad, barbed blade of the dagger, and its coiled body.

In the head are engraved the fourteen vowels from a to au, and below its body, the letters ha, ya, va, ra, la. The portion below is divided into 25 squares, arranged obliquely, and in each of the squares is to be seen the aksara, from ka to ma, know as sparsa, arranged in classes or vargas, five in each line. The portion below is shaped like a triangle, and in its right arm, which has four squares are engraved the aksara, sha, ssha, sa, ha, one in each square from top to bottom. The base is divided into four, each of which shows the jihumuliya, the upadhmaniya, the anusvara and the visarga, from left to right. In the left arm are engraved the aksara, ru, yu, u, from two to four, as the first letter in the first square has disappeared altogether. The loop that represents the tail is divided into 39 compartments, the compartments contain the terminations or nominal and verbal endings. (Not represented here).

Magic square

The magic square is the diamond in the Varnanaga-kripanika which contains all the sparsa or mute-consonants, 25 in all in a 5 × 5 grid. The Sanskrit alphabet is designed such that the difference between sounds of the sparsas is preserved whether you recite them horizontally (vargas) or vertically (ganas). It was extended and completed with frictives and sibilants, semi-vowels and vowels and was eventually codified into the Brahmi alphabet.

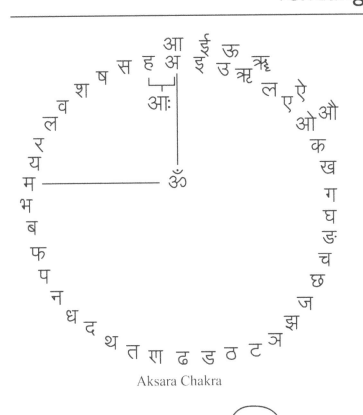

Aksara Chakra

1. a i u N — अ इ उ ए्
2. rri lri K — ऋ ल क्
3. e o N — ए ओ ङ्
4. ai au C — ऐ औ च्
5. h y v r T — ह य व र ट्
6. l N — ल ग्
7. n m n n n M — ञ म ङ ण न म्
8. jh bh N — झ भ ञ्
9. gh ddh dh S — घ ढ थ ष्
10. j b g dd d — ज ब ग ड द स्
11. kh ph ch tth th ca tt t V — ख फ छ ठ थ च ट त व्
12. k p Y — क प य्
13. s s a R — श ष स र्
14. h L — ह ल्

14 verses of the Meshasvara or Shiva Sutra

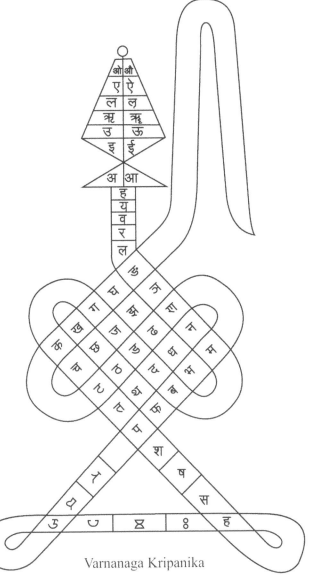

Varnanaga Kripanika

ka	kha	ga	gha	nga
ca	cha	ja	jha	nya
tta	ttha	dda	ddha	nna
ta	tha	da	dha	na
pa	pha	ba	bha	ma

क	ख	ग	घ	ङ
च	छ	ज	झ	ञ
ट	ठ	ड	ढ	ण
त	थ	द	ध	न
प	फ	ब	भ	म

grammatic magic square

Calligraphy and Typography

Unlike China, Japan or the Islamic world, traditional Indian calligraphy never acheived the level of a major art form, because of the low status given to writing by the Vedic Brahmins. There being no status or standardisation, scribes used many local variant letter forms in their often, miscopied, incorrectly spelt texts. This is one reason why Indian calligraphy has evolved many major script forms over the centuries.

Because of the high status given to the spoken word, Hindu's never truly created a religious script, as both Sanskrit and Prakrit were used as religious languages but were written in the national or local script. The only Indic script to truly achieve a sacred status was the formal variant of the Late Gupta-Brahmi script called Siddhamatrka. Venerated in China, Japan and Tibet, where written Sanskrit became more important than spoken Sanskrit.

The Gupta period 3rd – 6th c CE. was the height of Buddhism in India, and Buddhist education during this era began with a primer of 12 chapters which dealt with the letters of the alphabet and the ten thousand combinations of vowels and consonants. Before copying out the letters for the pupils the teacher wrote the word Siddham for them to copy. It comes from the root word 'sidh' which means acomplished, succesful, perfected.

Writing materials

Writing materials on the Indian subcontinent have influenced and transformed the calligraphic character of Brahmi script. Letters have been inscribed into or written onto various mediums such as stone, clay, metal, cotton cloth, birch bark and palm leaves, using various writing implements including the pointed stylus, feather, reed brush and square-cut nibbed pen. Around 500 BCE, wooden boards painted black and written on with chalk were used as teaching aids. Between 400 and 300 BCE, writing appeared on polished cotton cloth using a brush or bamboo pen and gum ink. Paper did not arrive on the continent till the 11th century CE. In certain parts of Indonesia, scripts styles were defined by the cutting of notches and points into bamboo with a knife.

In central and northern India people made books using treated Birch bark or Palm leaves, oiled and polished until hard enough to write on with a square-nibbed reed pen and gum ink. Although palm leaves do not absorb ink as paper does, gum ink remains on the surface of the leaf. In southern India, writing envolved inscribing letters into palm leaves using a special sharpened tool called a stylus. Once written, lamp black, coal dust or gum ink, is rubbed into the characters to make them visable when the excess is wiped away. The pages of a book were held together by a cord that ran through the holes in the middle of the leaves, finished with a wooden cover, if needed. The Grantha or knotted script of southern India takes its name from the book making process. Chinese and Japanese calligraphers abandoned the pen in favour of the brush when writing the Siddham script on paper made from the bark of the Mulberry tree.

Calligraphic styles

The use of different writing materials created script styles consisting of letters with differing stoke widths. In northern India, the use of the pen dipped in gum ink to write Indo-Aryan languages on birch bark or cotton cloth, created a modular stroke of thin and thick lines giving a visual character to the script. This led to the rise of different caligraphic forms, producing angular or square scripts like Devanagari, created using a thick nibbed bamboo pen and Ranjana, written with a feather. The cursive Saddham script was written in India with a pen, in China and Japan it was written with a brush.

In comparison, the use of the sharped metal stylus in southern India to write Dravidian languages, resulted in the creation of rounded, monolinear, letter forms that lack the straight and angular lines which splits the palm leaf. This rounded script style was used to write the Pali Cannon of Theraveda Buddhism and became the calligraphic inspiration for the national scripts of Burma, Thailand, Cambodia and Laos, and the island scripts of Indonesia.

Printing and Typography

Printing in India began in 1556 with Jesuit priests who brought a printing press to Goa before taking it to Ethiopia, but the Govenor-General requested it remained in Goa, where it was used by Christian missonaries to publish Biblical literature. In 1621 the Dutch East India company received 25 miles of eastern coast line called Torangambadi, where many mono colour hand press type machines served the area, printing was revived and spread throughout India.

Between 1818 and 1854, saw the publication of daily newspapers in Indian languges and Indian moveable typefaces based on calligraphic scripts – Bengali, Gujarati, Devanagari, Malayalam, Marathi, Tamil, Urdu and Telugu. These script types remained the norm in publishing until the advent of electronic font design in the 1970's, allowing Indian typographers to create more modern forms of all the major Brahmi script variants for print and screen. The modular appearence of southern Indian scripts is an influence of letterpress printing, which has been so great that a non-Roman intiative is being applied by todays Indian typographers.

The introduction of lithographic book printing to India made it cheaper to continue to employ scribes to write the text than the more expensive letterpress method of book production, as the large amount of individual characters contained in the Brahmi abugida made letterpress printing expensive. The advent of printing, has led to a gradual decline in the use of historic, liturgical scripts such as Grantha, due to a two pronged attack. Initialy from evangelical Christians who used the printing press to churn out tonnes of Christian literature. In an effort to address this, the Hindu elite set up their own presses, leading to the prevalentcy of Devanagari for the mass printing of books in Sanskrit. In some instances this has given rise to greater literacy in Indian society.

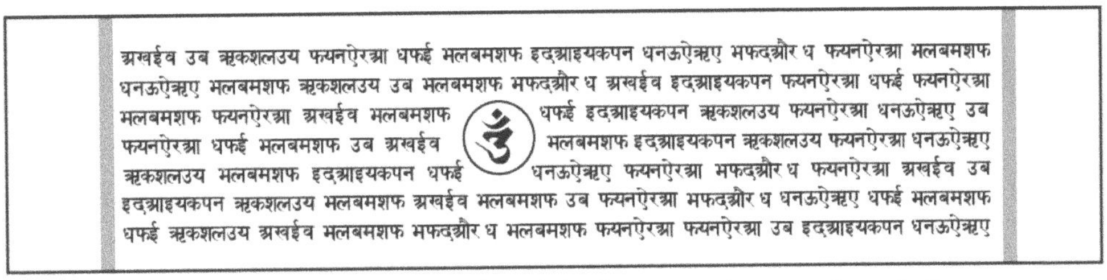

square-cut nibbed pen and birch bark manuscript - northern India

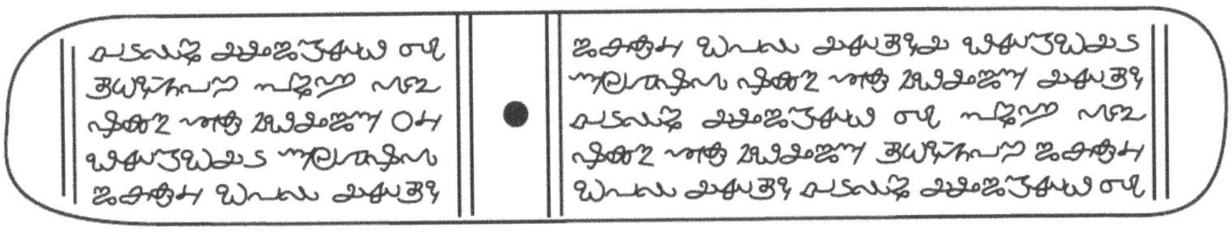

pointed stylus and palm leaf manuscript - southern India

book forms

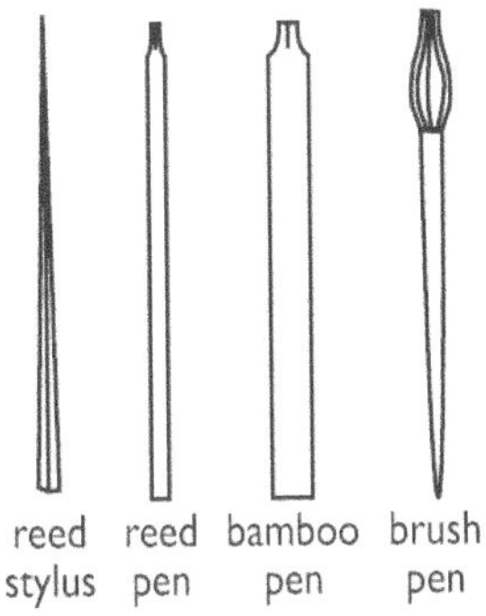
reed stylus
reed pen
bamboo pen
brush pen

writing implements

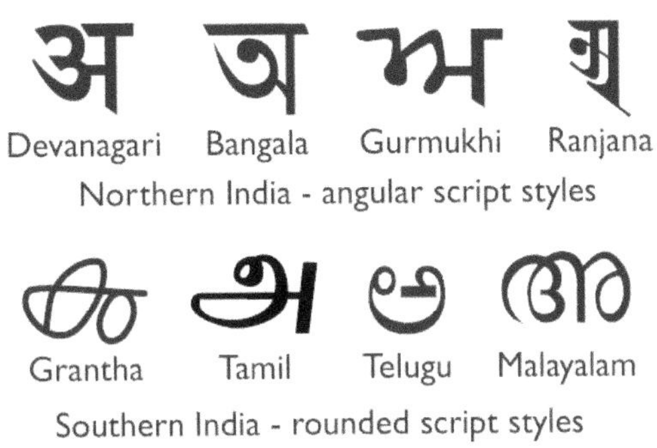
अ
Devanagari
Bangala
Gurmukhi
Ranjana
Northern India - angular script styles
Grantha
Tamil
Telugu
Malayalam
Southern India - rounded script styles

script variation in Indian calligraphy

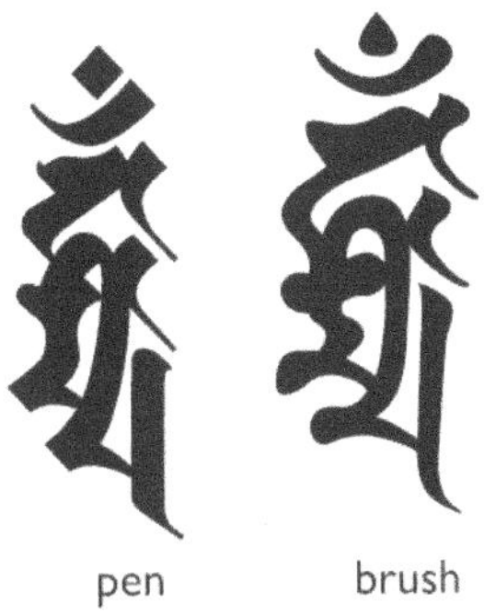
pen
brush

Siddham script

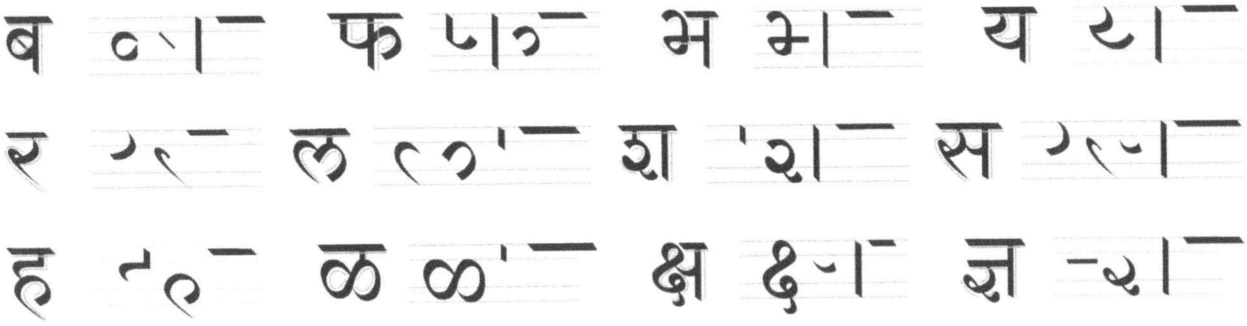
ब
फ
भ
य
र
ल
श
स
ह
ळ
क्ष
ज्ञ

caligraphic strokes for Devanagari script

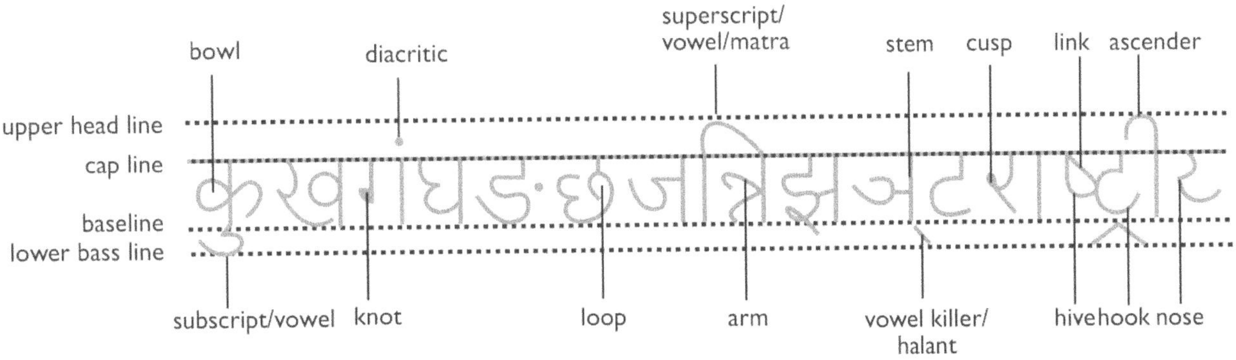
bowl
diacritic
superscript/ vowel/matra
stem
cusp
link
ascender
upper head line
cap line
baseline
lower bass line
subscript/vowel
knot
loop
arm
vowel killer/ halant
hive
hook
nose

elements of Indian typography

Script Family

The Brahmi script family is the largest script family in the world. Consisting of over fifty old and new scripts that, over the centuries have been used to write the speech of four different language groups from Pakistan to the Philippines. Its phonetic structure is alpha-syllabic and as a writing system it is mostly associated with the Devanagari script of India.

Most Indian scripts are primarily associated with the language for which they first evolved, (e.g. Gujarati) others have been given names referring to places (e.g. Nandinagari – southern Nagari), empires (e.g. Gupta, Pallava), scripts for writing texts in Sanskrit, (e.g. Grantha meaning book, Devanagari meaning divine script of the city), religious affiliations (e.g. Gurmukhi meaning from the mouth of the guru, the script of the Sikhs) or particular inscriptions (e.g. Siddham-ratsu meaning let there be perfection, written at the beginning of books.)

Indic scripts can be easily divided into two distinct groups; northern Brahmi characterized by a the use of an extended headline from which the letters hang to form words, made possible by the use of a square cut nibbed pen on prepared tree bark that allows the creation of straight lines; southern Brahmi is characterized by the use of a cursive, linear script written with a pointed stylus on prepared palm leaves that splits with the use of straight lines.

Brahmi lipi

The story of the Brahmi lipi or script begins with the undeciphered pictographic script of the Indus valley civilization. From the disappearance of the Indus script to the creation of Brahmi script, scant examples of lettering or writing are found only in South India and Sri Lanka. It is unknown if these examples had an influence on the creation of the Brahmi script.

The first proto-Brahmi script was written around 500 BCE in the city of Bhattiprolu in Andhra Pradesh. There are also examples of Tamil-Brahmi dated back to the 3rd c. BCE. The use of Brahmi lipi only spread throughout India from 250 BCE under the patronage of the King Asoka, the first Buddhist monarch of India and founder of the Mauryan empire.

Asoka commissioned the script to propagate his Buddhist edits across his empire. Asoka also commissioned a second script, Kharosthi used in the north western part of the Murayan empire to write his edicts in Indo-Batric and Greek. Brahmi lipi began to diversify into northern and southern varieties around 100 BCE.

Northern Brahmi

After the dissolution of the Muaryan kingdom, first the Kusan (2nd BCE-3rd CE) then the Gupta (300-600 CE) dynasties ruled northern India. Brahmi lipi changed only slightly during those reigns with the Kushan and Gupta variants named after them. The straight nibbed pen came into use leading to calligraphic diversity in thick and thin letter strokes, as well as calligraphic embellishment of the letter forms. In central India the use of the pen led to the emergence of script styles such as, nail and box headed styles which would influence the calligraphic style of northern scripts.

Towards the end of the Gupta era (700 CE), western and eastern variants of Gupta and two calligraphic forms called Kutila and Siddhamatrika, emerged to become the source scripts for the majority of regional or localized scripts across northern India – Sarada, Nagari, Bengali, Ranjana, all developed during the medieval period (8th-11thc.) to become the parents of Brahmi-derived scripts used to write the languages of northern India. In China and Japan, the formal version of the Late Gupta script achieved sacred script status, called Siddhamatrka 'perfected mothers' and Bonji meaning 'Sanskrit letters' in Japanese.

In the 16th and 17th centuries, clerks and merchants influenced the development of calligraphic cursive script styles such as Kaithili, Gujarati and Modi scripts. Following Indian independence in 1947, the Devanagari and Bangla scripts became the most commonly used writing systems of northern India.

Southern Brahmi

In southern India, The Andhra dynasty arose to power after the Maurayan. They were succeeded by the Kadambas, Pallavas, Chalukayas, Rastrakutas, Cholas and Pandyas. During those early dynasties, there developed a southern Brahmi style called Kadamba-Pallava, that diverged into two separate scripts in the 5th century. Kadamba became the source script for the Kannada, Telugu and Tulu scripts. Pallava became the source script for other south Indian scripts and, as a consequence, those southeast Asian writing systems referred to as Pali lipi.

From Tamil-Brahmi, the Tamil speaking Pallavas developed the cursive Vatteluttu script for writing Tamil in the 11th century. The Pallavas also developed a formal script from Vattelutu called Grantha "book", employed exclusively to write Sanskrit. A later eastern variant called Tamil-Grantha is the parent of modern Tamil. Through the centuries, Tamils used Grantha to write Tamil words in Sanskrit inscriptions until the script became used to write both Sanskrit and Tamil. The western variant of Grantha called Tigalari was used to write Tulu and Malayalam, before the Tulu was written in the Telugu script. Malayalam evolved into an independent script that inspired the Sinhala script of Sri Lanka.

Pali Lipi

Between the 3rd and 8th centuries CE. the Southern Brahmi scripts became the source of most of the scripts developed in the Hindu and Buddhist kingdoms of southeast Asia, Indonesia and the Philippines. Pyu is considered to be the parent of the Mon, Burmese, Lanna and Shan scripts. The elaborate Grantha script styles of the Tamil speaking Pallavas became the inspiration for the Khmer, Thai, Lao, Viet, Malay, Indonesian, Sumatran and the Philippino scripts. In Indonesia, some regional script styles are characterized by notches and points from the cutting of letters into bamboo with a knife

Script Family

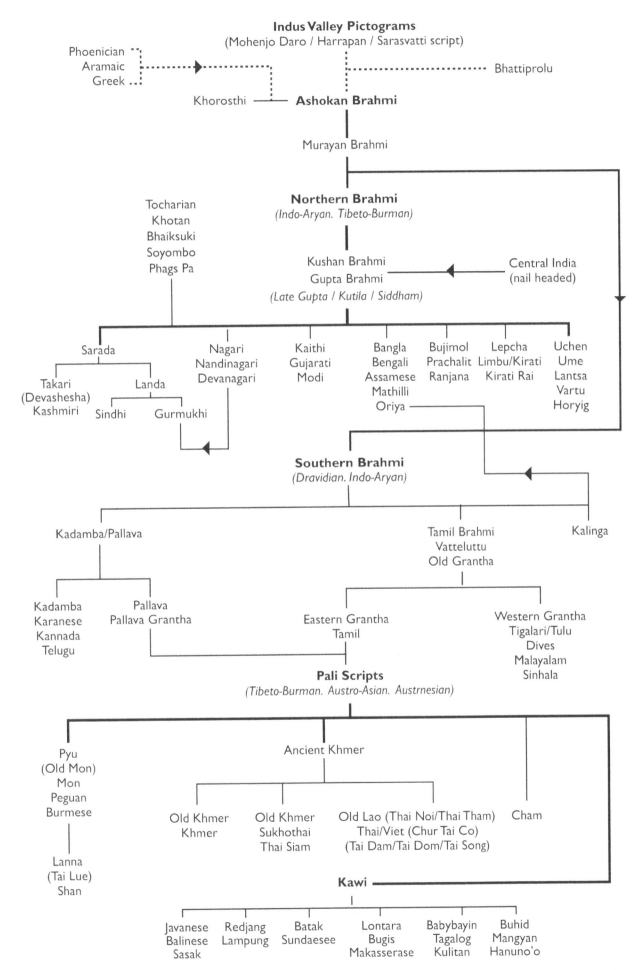

Indus Valley Pictograms
(Mohenjo Daro / Harrapan / Sarasvatti script)

Phoenician
Aramaic
Greek

Bhattiprolu

Khorosthi —— **Ashokan Brahmi**

Murayan Brahmi

Northern Brahmi
(Indo-Aryan. Tibeto-Burman)

Tocharian
Khotan
Bhaiksuki
Soyombo
Phags Pa

Kushan Brahmi
Gupta Brahmi
(Late Gupta / Kutila / Siddham)

Central India
(nail headed)

Sarada

Nagari
Nandinagari
Devanagari

Kaithi
Gujarati
Modi

Bangla
Bengali
Assamese
Mathilli
Oriya

Bujimol
Prachalit
Ranjana

Lepcha
Limbu/Kirati
Kirati Rai

Uchen
Ume
Lantsa
Vartu
Horyig

Takari
(Devashesha)
Kashmiri

Landa

Sindhi   Gurmukhi

Southern Brahmi
(Dravidian. Indo-Aryan)

Kadamba/Pallava

Tamil Brahmi
Vatteluttu
Old Grantha

Kalinga

Kadamba
Karanese
Kannada
Telugu

Pallava
Pallava Grantha

Eastern Grantha
Tamil

Western Grantha
Tigalari/Tulu
Dives
Malayalam
Sinhala

Pali Scripts
(Tibeto-Burman. Austro-Asian. Austrnesian)

Pyu
(Old Mon)
Mon
Peguan
Burmese

Ancient Khmer

Lanna
(Tai Lue)
Shan

Old Khmer
Khmer

Old Khmer
Sukhothai
Thai Siam

Old Lao (Thai Noi/Thai Tham)
Thai/Viet (Chur Tai Co)
(Tai Dam/Tai Dom/Tai Song)

Cham

Kawi

Javanese
Balinese
Sasak

Redjang
Lampung

Batak
Sundaesee

Lontara
Bugis
Makasserase

Babybayin
Tagalog
Kulitan

Buhid
Mangyan
Hanuno'o

Indus Valley Script

The Indus valley civilization evolved along the banks of the Indus river that flows between Pakistan and northwest India, in north Sindh and south Punjab. At its peak, between 2500 and 1900 BCE, the major cities of the Indus Valley ranked alongside those of Mesopotamia and Egypt. Prior to its discovery in 1921, no-one had even suspected the existence of such a civilization in India. This archaic civilization disappeared around 1900 BCE, 300 years before the arrival of Aryan speaking people from Iran who became the Hindu's of India.

The noun India, is derived from the local appellation for the people of the Indus Valley and beyond. In Sanskrit it is Sindhu, in Persian it is Hindu, in Greek its is Indus and in English it is India. India's ancient name for itself was Bharatavarsha, named after a legendry ancient emperor. Its modern name has been shortened to 'Barat'.

Indus Valley script

The Indus valley script is the usual name given to the pictographic system employed by the ancient people whose culture was established along the banks of the Indus river. More recently, the script has been called Mohen-jo-Darro script and Harappan script after the people of the area. Even more recently it has been termed the Sarasvati script after the river and area where most of the artifacts have been found.

About 3500 Indus valley inscriptions are known. They were found carved onto seal stones, pottery, copper tablets, bronze implements and bone and ivory rods. The Indus valley inscriptions are brief, the average has less than four signs to a line and five signs in a text. The longest inscription is only 20 signs in three lines.

Scholars tend to agree that there are about 400 Indus signs in all (plus or minus 25). This means that there are too many signs to be an alphabet or syllabary. Leading to the conclusion that it must be a mixed script of pictograms and logograms like the scripts of Egypt and Mesopotamia.

The Indus script still defies decipherment because the language spoken in the ancient Indus valley is not known. Although linguists now think the Indus people spoke a mixed language of Austro-Asian and Dravidian. Due to this, it looks unlikely that the script will ever be deciphered, as many of its signs are so simplified and schematic that their pictorial meaning is difficult to perceive. Condemning it to remain an unknown script, writing a unknown language.

Easter Island script (Rongo-rongo)

Rongo-rongo script is a an undeciphered script of an unknown language, but the Indus script may be its parent, as certain Indus pictogram bear a striking resemblance to signs found in on Easter Island. The pictograms may be only two centuries old, or they may have travelled over from the Indus to the Pacific islands, over 13,000 miles of ocean away, over a period of 3500 years.

Tamil

Since independence, Tamil scholars have claimed that their ancient history, as the descendents of the Indus Valley civilisation has been usurped, first by the Hindu's and reiterated by the British. These scholars claim that they can trace the Tamil script back to the Indus valley and that the present Tamil script is a direct descendent of that ancient script.

They claim Indus Valley inscriptions are written in Tamil in a syllabic writing system similar to Elamite writing and proto-Sumerian seals. With many scholars now claiming the bulk of Vedic, Brahmin and Hindu philosophies and texts are originally from the Indus Valley people. Both the worship of Shiva and the practise of yoga are thought to have originated in the Indus valley. This includes the phonetic system used to formulate Sanskrit and the script to write it. Tamil scholars claim the Brahmi script evolved from the studies in phonemics, which the Dravidians had specialised in, and is completely phonetic.

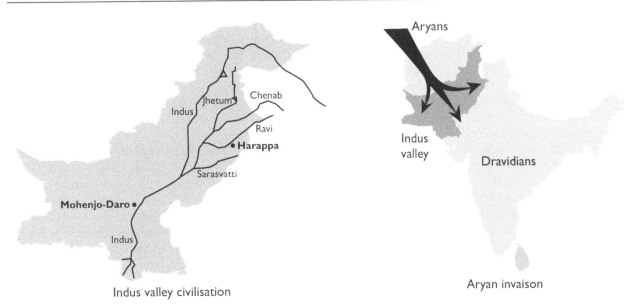

ancient Indus civilisation of Pakistan

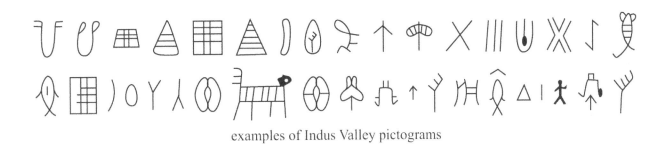

examples of Indus Valley pictograms

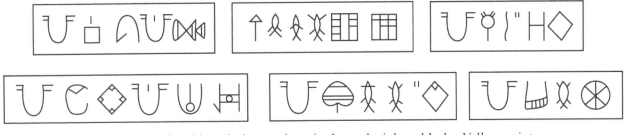

specimens of seal inscriptions written in the undeciphered Indus Valley script

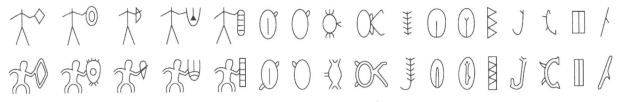

Indus valley - top, Rong-rongo - bottom

similiarities between Indus valley and Easter island scripts

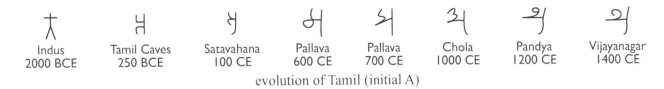

| Indus | Tamil Caves | Satavahana | Pallava | Pallava | Chola | Pandya | Vijayanagar |
| 2000 BCE | 250 BCE | 100 CE | 600 CE | 700 CE | 1000 CE | 1200 CE | 1400 CE |

evolution of Tamil (initial A)

Asokan Edicts

Proper writing on the Indian subcontinent was really a Buddhist initiative. Vedic Brahmanism was a oral religion that revered the learning and correct pronunciation of the Sanskrit language for religious ritual, and did not value the writing of religious texts for that reason.

Following the split from Vedic Brahmanism, Buddha himself recognized the importance of the written word when transmitting his teachings. The Jains also took the same stance when it came to propagating their own doctrines. Buddha declared that his words should be written as he spoke them in his native tongue. Buddha spoke Magdhi Prakrit but the orthodox teachings of Buddha are written in Pali Prakrit. This is because Pali is later version of Magdhi. He also declared that where possible his teachings should be written in the local language or dialect.

In the south, this occurred through the orthodox Theraveda school of Buddhism, or Hinayana Buddhism meaning "little vehicle," giving rise to the spread of the Indian writing system across southern India and southeast Asia. In north India, the Himalayas, and east Asia, the mystical doctrines of Mahayana Buddhism or the "great vehicle, propagated Buddhist and Tantric texts written in Sanskrit. By 12th century CE Buddhism was no longer practised in India.

Asokan Brahmi

In 642 BCE, the kingdom of Magdha was founded in the Ganges plain by Sisunga. By the fourth century BCE, the Indo-Aryan heartland had moved from the Indus to the Ganges. In the Ganges plain, the kingdom of Magdha, one among many contending kingdoms and states, had emerged, pre-eminent in size and strength. In 370 BCE, Magdha was consolidated as an empire by king Nanda, creating India' first non-kshatriya ruling dynasty. Although his dynasty lasted only 50 years he qualifies as India's first emperor.

In 322 BCE, the Nanda dynasty was overthrown by the Muarya dynasty. They expanded Magdha into India's first great empire, covering most of greater India. Around the middle of the 3rd century BCE, India's first Buddhist King, Asoka Muarya commissioned the creation of two scripts to propagate his Buddhist edicts across the empire.

The Asokan edicts appeared between 253 and 250 BCE, inscribed in stone across India, Bangladesh, Nepal, Pakistan and Afghanistan, written in Magdhi Prakrit, Gandhara Prakrit and Indo-Batric languages, using two scripts, Brahmi and Kharosthi, as well as in Greek and Aramaic. The origin of the Indian scripts is hotly debated. Some scholars believing that the scripts, especially the Kharosthi script are derived from western alphabets such as Aramaic, South Semitic, Greek or Phoenician, as it shares some characteristics of these forms of alphabetic scripts.

Other scholars believe the Brahmi script is in fact an Indian invention separate to the western alphabetic script. Theorizing that Brahmi script developed from the Harappan script of the Indus valley, although anyone has yet to prove this. Examples of proto-Brahmi script that date to 500 BCE with short inscription in copper exist but these are scarce.

Employed throughout the empire by Asoka, Brahmi or Lett as it was known at that time, was a linear script of stylized graphemes or letter-signs representing five independent vowels, four vowel markers and 31 consonants with an inherent vowel sound 'a', to write Magdhi Prakrit. At first it was written right to left in the Semitic style before being written left to right as it is today.

These inscriptions are generally considered to be the oldest of Indian scripts. Asoka's edicts established writing as a medium of expression among the diverse segments of the population and provided the impetus for the diffusion of the divine alphabet throughout Asia.

Kharosthi

Around 533 BCE, Cyrus the Great, ruler of the Persian empire began to extract tribute from the kingdoms of Kamboja and Gandhara in Pakistan. As a result of the infusion of Persian influence into the subcontinent, the Aramaic script was introduced into the northwest India.

The Kharosthi script was commissioned by Asoka at the same time as the Brahmi script. In Pakistan and Afghanistan, Asoka's edicts were written in Magadhi Prakrit, Gandhara Prakrit and Indo-Batric, using the Kharosthi script. Kharosthi is a district of Gandhara, and the script became known as Kharosthi or Gandhari, as well as Indo-Batric. It was widely used in northwest India and Central Asia from the time of Asoka until the fourth century CE when it died out leaving no descendents.

Although nothing is known about its origin, it is generally thought to be derived from the Aramaic script. Its written direction from right to left, as well as similarities with Aramaic letter forms support this assumption. At the time Aramaic was the most important administrative language used from Syria to Afghanistan, it seems likely that the northern Indian empire borrowed the Aramaic script. It was also used in the Kushana empire and Sogdiana, an ancient Iranian civilization and along the Silk road, which is how Buddhism and the Brahmi script reached Mongolia, China and Japan.

Asokan Edicts

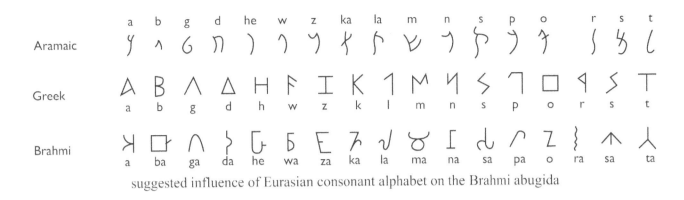

suggested influence of Eurasian consonant alphabet on the Brahmi abugida

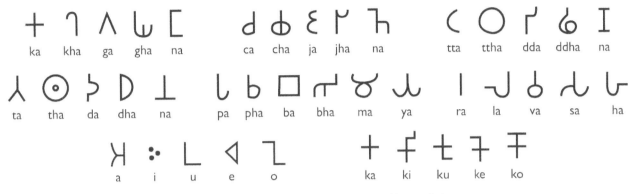

Ashokan Brahmi abugida for Magdha Prakrit

syllables, vowels and diacritics for the Indo-Bactrian, Kharosthi script

suggested influence of Semitic consonant script on Indo-Bactrian syllabic script

Kharosthi script

Brahmi Lipi

The origin of Brahmi lipi or Brahmi script is disputed. Some scholars perceive that Brahmi lipi is a native Indian invention separate to the western alphabet. Theorizing the Brahmi script evolved from the Harappan script of the Indus valley, although anyone has yet to prove this. The earliest examples of Brahmi lipi are found in Anuradhapura, Sri Lanka, with short inscription in copper and on broken pottery, dated between the 6th to the 4th century BCE, but these are scarce.

Just like the Greek alphabet, it had many local variants, which suggests that its origin lies father back in time. Circumstantial evidence points to merchants using a business script for at least one hundred years prior to the Asokan edicts, and there are allusions in literary sources, dating from the 6th c. BCE, but transcribed later.

Brahmi Lipi was sparingly utilized, if at all, until the advent of Buddhism and to a lesser extent Jainsim. Buddha insisted his teachings be given to all people in their own language. King Asoka's conversion to Buddhism created the edicts which are written in Magdhi Prakrit, a common form of Sanskrit and the native tongue of Buddha.

Over the millennia, Brahmi lipi has undergone certain transformations. From the proto-Brahmi scripts of Bhattiprolu and Tamil, to its standardization and institution as Asokan Brahmi, into a dynastic Muaryan variant which can be divided into two stages, Uttari, ancient and Daksimi, modern. By the 6th century CE, the modern form had evolved into northern and southern variants which would be the inspiration for the modern scripts of the Indian sub-continent.

At the time of its creation, Brahmi lipi was called Leth or Lett, the name Brahmi is said to have come from a Jain legend. According to South Indian myth, a Jain monk called Vrushabhadeva explained the script to his daughters, Brahmi and Soundhary. Therefore as a mark of this, the writing script is called Brahmi and the numerals are called Soundhary.

According to Tamil tradition, the Brahmi letter shapes were formed on a grid or from basic geometric shapes, complying with phonetic rationales. There are three ideas of what the signs are based on. First, a pictographic source based on Indus Valley script, in which the pictograms have been rotated 90 degress to produce letters. Second, that the letter forms are based on the position of the speech organs during pronunciation, transcribed into geometric forms.

Lastly, the signs are produced by Cymatics, the study of the inter relationship of sound and form. Hans Jenny discovered that when the sounds of the Vedic alphabet are spoken, the written form of the sound appears in sand placed on a resonator plate, or in an electron vibration field sensor called a Tonoscope. The sound of the letter is the vibratory form of that letter.

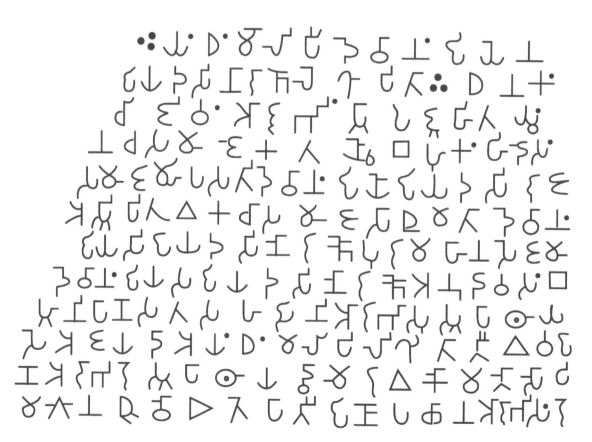

Ashoka's first edict

Brahmi Lipi

| a | i | u | e | o | ka | kha | ga | gha | ca | cha | ja | jha | tta | ttha | dda | ddha |

| ta | tha | da | dha | na | pa | pha | ba | bha | ma | ya | ra | la | va | sa | sa | sa | ha |

pre-Brahmic Tamil/Indus script

| a | i | u | e | o | ka | kha | ga | gha | na | ca | cha | ja | jha | na |

| tta | ttha | dda | ddha | na | ta | tha | da | dha | na | pa | pha | ba | bha | ma | ya | ra | la | va | sa | ha |

geometric letter forms

| a | i | u | e | o | ka | kha | ga | gha | na | ca | cha | ja | jha | na | tta | ttha | dda | ddha | na |

| ta | tha | da | dha | na | pa | pha | ba | bha | ma | ya | ra | la | va | sa | ha |

cursive letter forms

| a | aa | i | ii | u | uu | e | oo | am | ka | kha | ga | gha | ca | cha | ja | na | tta | ttha | dda | ddha | na |

| ta | tha | da | dha | na | pa | pha | ba | ma | ya | ra | la | va | sa | sa | sa | ha |

Mauryan Brahmi

Northern Brahmi

Between 100 and 600 CE, the Brahmi script slowly diversified into distinguishable northern and southern variants. In northern India, variants of the Bramhi abugida are used to write the major Indo-Aryan languages of Sanskrit, Hindi, Punjabi, Sindhi, Gujarati, Bengali, Assamese, Marathi and Oriya as well as other languages and dialects.

The scripts of northern India slowly evolved through successive dynastic variants. From the Brahm lipi of the Muaryan empire, 4th – 1st century BCE, through the Middle Brahmi of the Kushan dynasty, 1st c. BC – 3rd c. CE, to the Late Brahmi script of the Gupta dynasty, 3rd – 5th century CE. After the 6th century, the Late Gupta script evolved western and eastern variants, which influenced the character of the regionalized medieval scripts, which replaced the Late Gupta Brahmi script across northern India by the 10th century.

Kushana Brahmi

The Kushan script of 100 BCE to 300 CE, is referred to as middle Brahmi. Following the break up of the Mauryan empire, new kingdoms evolved. In central India, the Shatavahana dynasty established a powerful empire in the Deccan. In the north, nomadic tribes of Mongol and Turkic heritage invaded through the Indus valley to create the Shaka and Kushan empires.

During the Kushan dynasty, the introduction of a new writing tool, the straight edged pen and an increase of writing by private individuals, brought variation to the Brahmi lipi. This led to a variety of skilled and unskilled script styles, since local scribes were employed to write the inscriptions of that particular locality. The use of the straight edged pen made the vertical portion thick at the top and gradually thin towards the bottom, giving a dagger like shape to the letters. The pen was also responsible for the flourish and thickened top found in the curves of the letters.

From the 1st century CE onwards, the development of the head-mark, a distinguishing feature, is noticed during the next two or three hundred years. These head-marks, deliberately made by the scribes, are distinguished as (1) the line head-mark, which replaced the tapering one of the earlier period. (2) the block head-mark, (3) the notched head-mark, (4) solid square head-mark, (5) hollow square head-mark, (6) solid triangle head-mark. Use of the striaght edged pen also led to the development of other calligraphic features such as tails, loops and hooks, all of which became characteristic features of Gupta script.

Gupta Brahmi

The successor to Kushan Brahmi is called Gupta Brahmi, developed between 300 and 500 CE, named after the ruling dynasty of that period. Early Gupta retained old Kushan forms while introducing some new letter forms, particularly with the letter 'i'. Used to write Sanskrit, it had some influence in the creation of the so-called Pali scripts of southeast Asia.

After the 6th c.CE. Gupta Brahmi acquired the name 'Kutila' meaning crooked, bent, angular, stemming from the right-angled, downward, finishing stroke at the end of a letter stem, created with by a twist of the pen. This style is best seen in the calligraphy of Nepalese Moll and the Devanagari derived Ranjana script used in Nepal and Tibet.

The late form of Gupta Brahmi became the parent of all the regional script styles of northern India. This was made possible by the use of a formal version of the script, that by the end of the 7th century CE had became known as Siddham or Siddhamatrika. The Sarada, Devanagari and Bangla evolved out of the western and eastern variants of the formal Gupta Brahmi script called Siddhamatrka.

During the Gupta era, Buddhism was at its height in India and the formal Gupta Brahmi or Siddhamatrka was used to write the Buddhists manuscripts that travelled along the Silk road to China and Japan. Outside India, Siddhamatrka became revered, employed as a sacred script to write Sanskrit and mantras in China and Japan, where it is still practiced.

Muarya

Kushana

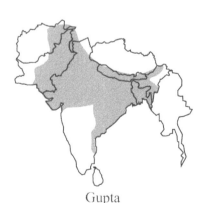

Gupta

Northern Brahmi

| Ashokan 3th c. bce | Kusnan 2th c. bce | Gupta 4th c. ce | Late Gupta 6-12th c. ce | Sharada 9th c. ce | Nagari 11-12th c. ce | Bangla 10-12th c. ce | Modern Sharada 14th c. ce |

development of northern script styles for the independent vowel A

| a | i | e | u | o | ka | kha | ga | gha | ca | cha | ja | jha | tta | ttha | dda | ddha | na |

| ta | tha | da | dha | ne | pa | ba | bha | ma | ya | ra | la | va | sa | sa | sa | ha |

Kushana Brahmi

| Brahmi *linear* | Dagger script | Nail headed | Box headed | Kutila *crooked/bent* | Nagari *headed* |

central and northern calligraphic forms

| a | i | u | e | ka | kha | ga | gha | na | ca | cha | ja | na | tta | dda | ta |

| tha | da | dha | na | pa | pha | ba | bha | ma | ya | ra | la | va | sa | sa | sa | ha |

Early Gupta

| a | aa | i | ii | u | uu | ri | rri | li | lli | e | ai | o | au | am | ah |

| ka | kha | ga | gha | na | ca | cha | ja | jha | na | tta | ttha | dda | ddha | na |

| ta | tha | da | dha | na | ba | bha | ma | ya | ra | la | va | sa | sa | sa | ha | lla | ksha |

Late Gupta - western variant

| a | aa | i | ii | u | e | ai | o |

| ka | kha | ga | gha | ca | cha | ja | na | tta | ttha | dda | ddha | na |

| ta | tha | da | dha | na | pa | pha | ba | bha | ma | ya | ra | sa | la |

Late Gupta - eastern variant

Siddhamatrka

Siddhamatrka is the name given to a calligraphic refinement of the northern Brahmi variant called Late Gupta script, from which the later Sarada, Nagari and Bangala scripts are descended. Siddhamatrka was employed to write Sanskrit texts between the 6th and 13th centuries CE. It was a formal style created by writing Gupta Brahmi with a squre-nibbed, bamboo pen, to form the capital letters individually in Indian ink on manuscripts made of birch bark, or more commonly palm leaves. The leaves or pages were gathered together, holes drilled into them and bound with string to create books.

The word Siddham became synonomous with Tantric Buddhism via the Late Gupta script. Buddhist education during this era began with a primer of 12 chapters, which delt with the letters of the alphabet and the ten thousand combinations of vowels and consonants. Before copying out the letters for the pupils, the teacher wrote the word 'Siddham' for them to copy. It comes from the root word 'sidh' which means 'accomplished, succesful, perfected.' The letters themselves are perfected, having been created by Brahma.

Alternatively, Siddhamratsu – may there be perfection, or Naviah Sarvajnaya Siddham – homage to the all knowing perfection, were written at the head of a book or letter list. This how the word Siddham became synonomous with the letters and the primer. As an invocation, Om Swasti Siddham, is used before the beginning of alphabets. The practice of invocation is still followed on the occasion of Yajoopavit Sanskar or religious chord wearing ceremony, when a young student writes alphabets on a wooden plank or takhti. The famous traveller Alberuni gave it the name of Siddha-Matrika, meaning 'perfected mothers', relating to the alphabets Goddess status.

During the Gupta era, Buddhism was at its height in India and Sanskrit texts were transported along the Silk Road, making their way to China, Tibet and Japan. Buddhist Tantrics considered it important to preserve the Sanskrit pronunciation of mantras. Since Chinese characters are not suitable for translating Sanskrit, the use of the Siddham script was retained and preserved in East Asia, and the writing of Siddham survived where Tantric Buddhism persisted. Therefore more attention was paid to the letterforms of Siddham.

Outside of India, Tantric Buddhists abandoned the square-nibbed pen in favour of the brush and Siddham assumed its place in Asian calligraphy. Particular importance was placed on the faithful reproduction of bija and mantra composed in Siddham. In contrast to Devanagari in India, Siddham in China and Japan was never used for anything but sacred writing.

Following the annexation of trade and pilgrim routes by Islamic expansion in the 8th century, the practise of writing Siddham script was preserved and reached its zenith with the Shingon school of Buddhism, producing the largest number of Siddham master calligraphers. The most reknown being Kukai, aka Kobi Dashi, the monk who first introduced Siddhamatrka to Japan, bringing it back with him from China during the 9th century. Siddhamatrka is revered by Shingon Buddhists as 'Bonji' meaning 'Sanskrit script' or 'Buddhist characters', used to write out mantras and sutras in Sanskrit using a brush pen.

Today, none of the original Gupta texts in Siddhamatrka exist, only the Chinese and Japanese variants of this formal script are known. Since the 7th or 8th centuries, Siddhamatrka has been exclusively used for seed syllables or bija and mantras. Nothing original has been composed in the script in India, China, Tibet or Japan.

Siddhamatrka

a	aa	i	i	u	u	ri	rii

i	i	e	ai	o	au	am	ah

ka	kha	ga	gha	na	ca	cha	ja	jha	na

tta	ttha	dda	ddha	na	ta	tha	da	dha	na

pa	pha	ba	bha	ma	ya	ra	la	va

sa	sa	sa	ha	la	ksa

ka	kaa	ki	kii	ku	kuu	kri	krii	ke	kai	ko	kau

Siddhamatrka / Bonji

Siddhamrastu

Namah Sarvajnaya Siddham

Sarada

Sarada is a nearly extinct regional script employed in the northwest India states of Sindh (Pakistan), Punjab, Jammu and Kashmir, to write Sanskrit and Kashmiri. It is the parent of script of the Landa and Takkri, making it the grandparent of the Sindhi and Gurmukhi scripts.

Sarada (Sharada)

Sarada is another name for Sarasvatti, the river goddess of eloquence and poetry, wife of Brahma, the Creator God of knowledge. The script first emerged in Kashmir as a monumental, carved or incised script. It evolved from the northern Late Gupta Brahmi variant or Siddham script, during the second half of the 9th century CE. Being built on the same system, Sarada is allied with Nagari, but letter forms differ.

Originally used by the educated Hindu minority in Kashmir, it was the first regional script developed for writing Vedic texts in Sanskrit. (This probably qualifies Sarada as India's only true religious script). It evolved several variants to write Sanskrit, Punjabi and Kashmiri. Sarada is taught in schools but not used in printing books. Today, only a small group of Brahmins (Jyotishis and Puroluts) continue to use Sarada for writing and calculating astrological and ritual formulas (Panchangs and horoscopes). It is possible the script maybe come extinct.

Classic / Modern Sarada (Devashasha)

The Sharada script underwent slow changes in the characters until the beginning of the thirteenth century CE. Classic Sarada evolved in the 13th century, described as being the southern variant from Bombay. In the 15th century, the knobs and wedges of the classic Sarada script gave way to loops and triangles of modern Sarada, whose letterforms are nearly identical in form to their counterpart in classic Sarada. The term Devashasha is used to describe the change in the later Sarada script between the 13th and 15th centuries.

Kashmiri

The Kashmiri script is essentially a more modern version of the Sarada script. All the letters have nearly identical shape to their counterpart in modern Sarada. The language of Kashmiri is spoken in the Indian state of Jammu and Kashmir, as well as immediately nearby areas in both India and Pakistan. Typical of this politically charged area is that the Kashmiri language is spoken by both Hindus and Muslims, but each group would write the Kashmiri language with a different script. The use of the Kashmiri script to write the Kashmiri language is mostly confined to Hindus, while Muslims would write the Kashmiri language with the Perso-Arabic derived script, Nasta-liq, similar to that of Urdu.

अ अ य य य म

graphic development of independent A for Sharada lipi

अ	अ	ऊ	ऊ	उ	उ	ए	उ
a	aa	i	ii	u	uu	e	o

क	ख	ग	घ	ङ	च	छ	ज	झ	ण	ट	ठ	ड	ढ	ण
ka	kha	ga	gha	na	ca	cha	ja	jha	na	tta	ttha	dda	ddha	na

त	थ	द	ध	न	प	फ	ब	भ	म	य	र	ल	व	स	स	स	ह
ta	tha	da	dha	na	pa	pha	ba	bha	ma	ya	ra	la	va	sa	sa	sa	ha

Sarada 8th-10th century

a	aa	i	ii	u	uu	e	ai	o	au

ka	kha	ga	gha	n	ca	cha	ja	tta	ttha	dda	ddha	n	ta	tha

da	dha	n	pa	pha	bha	ma	ya	ra	la	va	sa	sa	sa	ha

Classic Sarada 10th -14th century

a	aa	i	ii	u	uu	r	ri	li	lii	e	ai	o	au

ka	kha	ga	gha	na	ca	cha	ja	jha	na	tta	ttha	dda	ddha	na	ta	tha

da	dha	na	pa	pha	ba	bha	ma	ya	ra	la	va	sa	sa	sa	ha

Modern Sarada 15th-19th century

a	aa	i	ii	u	uu	ri	rii	li	lii	e	ai	o	au	an	am	ah

ka	kha	ga	gha	na	ca	cha	ja	jha	na	tta	ttha	dda	ddha	na

tta	ttha	dda	ddha	na	pa	pha	ba	bha	ma	ya	ra	la	lla	va	sa	sa	sa	ha

Kashmiri 20th century

Gurmukhi

From the 8th century CE, the western form of the Late Gupta Brahmi evolved regional script variants. In the northwest of India (Kashmir, Punjab, Sindh (Pakistan) it was the parent to the Sarada script. This, in turn became the parent of other northwestern scripts called Landa and Takari. The Landa script became the parent of Sindhi and Gurmukhi, the sacred script of Sikhism.

Landa

The word Landa means "without tail." A variant of the Sarada script, becoming graphically distinct by the 10th century CE. It was primarily used in Punjab and Sindh to write the Punjabi language, but it was not well suited, due to additional sounds present in the Punjabi language. As a consequence, during the 16th century AD, the Landa script became the template for the Gurmukhi script, which was created to better represent the Punjabi language. There are also ten scripts that can be classified as Landa, mostly merchant scripts. Today it is used by a minority of family derived businesses to hide information from their customers.

Takri, Takari, Takakri. Tankri, Tankan

Takri is a Brahmic script which developed from the Sarada script in the 14th century. Related to Landa and Gurmukhi, it emerged as a distinct script in the 16th century. Employed as an official script in parts of northwest India between the 17th to the 20th century. Officially adopted in the 1860's, it was replaced by Devanagari and Arabic script after 1944.

There is considerable variation in the Takri alphabet with each state or region have its own version. A version of Takri was the official script of Chamba state, now in Himachal Pradesh. In Jammu and Kashmir, a version of Takri known as Dogri Akkhor was used to write the official language of Dogri. The origin of the name is uncertain. It may be derived from the word "tanka" meaning "coin", or that it is the script of the "Takkas", the old landed class of the Punjab.

Gurmukhi

The Gurmukhi script was invented in the 16th century by the second Sikh Guru, Guru Angad Dev, to replace the Landa script for writing the Punjabi language. It has also been adapted to write Braj, Bhasha, Sanskrit and Sindhi. With the penning of Guru Grantha Sahib's 1430 pages in Gurmukhi, it became the principal script of the Sikhs. The name comes from the old Punjabi word "guramukhi" translated as 'the script that issued from the mouth of the guru'. Originally derived from the Sarada variant Landa, mixed with influences from the Nagari script style.

Sindhi

In the mid 19th century, the Landa script was adopted to write Sindhi, an Indo-Aryan language spoken in the eastern province of Sindh in Pakistan. The Sindhi or Khudawadi script was decreed a standard script for Sindh in 1868. It was developed by Narayan Jagannath Mehta, the Deputy Educational Inspector in Sindh, and is based mainly on the old Khudawadi script, which was used in Hyderabad. It was officially known as the 'Hindi-Sindhi' script or 'Hindu-Sindhi', used in education and literature. However, this proved to be short lived, as Sindhi eventually became written in either Devanagari or Perso-Arabic script by the middle of the 20th century AD.

Gurmukhi

ੴ ॐ ਅ

from Sarada to Landa to Gurmukhi

੭	ਰ	੮	੨	ਨ	ੲ	ਮ	੮	੮	ਝ	੮	੮	੮	੮	੩
a	i	u	ka	kha	ga	gha	na	ca	cha	ja	jha	na	tta	ttha	dda

੮	੮	੩	੩	੮	੮	੮	੮	੮	੮	੩	੮	੮	੮	੮	੮	੮
ddha	na	ta	tha	da	dha	na	pa	pha	ba	bha	ma	ya	ra	la	va	ra	sa	ha

Landa

ਤ	ਤ	੮	੮	੮	੮	੮	੮	੮	੮
a	aa	i	ii	u	uu	e	ai	o	au

ਆ	ਖ	ਗ	ਘ	ਂ	ਜ	ਤ	ਤ	੮	੮	੮	੮	੮	੮	੮	੮
ka	kha	ga	gha	na	ca	cha	ja	jha	ta	tha	da	dha	na	tta	ttha	dda	ddha	na

ਪ	੮	੮	੮	੮	੮	੮	੮	੮	੮	੮	੮	੮	੮
pa	pha	ba	bha	ma	ya	ra	la	va	sa	sa	sa	ha	rra	lla

Takkri (Dogri)

ਅ	ਆ	ਇ	ਈ	ਉ	ਊ	ਏ	ਐ	ਓ	ਔ
a	a	i	i	u	u	e	ai	o	au

ਕ	ਖ	ਗ	ਘ	ਙ	ਚ	ਛ	ਜ	ਝ	ਞ
ka	kha	ga	gha	na	ca	cha	ja	jha	na

ਟ	ਠ	ਡ	ਢ	ਣ	ਤ	ਥ	ਦ	ਧ	ਨ
tta	ttha	dda	ddha	na	ta	tha	da	dha	na

ਪ	ਫ	ਬ	ਭ	ਮ	ਯ	ਰ	ਲ	ਵ	ੜ	ਸ	ਹ
pa	pha	ba	bha	ma	ya	ra	la	va	ra	sa	ha

ਗ਼	ੜ	ਸ	ੜ	ਲ	ੜ	ਸ	ਜ	ਲ	ੜ
gya	nha	mha	rha	lha	rha	sa	za	la	tr

Gurmukhi

ਅ	ਆ	ੲ	ੲ	ੳ	ੳ	ਐ	ਐ	ਐ	ਐ
a	aa	i	ii	u	uu	e	ai	o	au

ਨ	੮	੮	੮	੮	੮	੮	੮	੮	੮	੮	੮	੮	੮	੮	੮	੮	੮
ka	kha	ga	ga	gha	na	ca	cha	ja	ja	jha	na	tta	ttha	dda	dda	dha	na	ra	ta	tha	da

੮	੮	੮	੮	W	੮	੮	੮	੮	੮	੮	੮	੮	੮	੮	੮	੮
dha	na	pa	pha	ba	bha	ma	ya	ra	la	wa	sha	sa	ha	qa	kha	ga	za	fa

Sindi

Devanagari

The most influential and most widely used of all northern Brahmi scripts, Nagari is the forerunner of the Devanagari script. It began as a regional script style used across central and northern India. Like its sister script, Bangla, it evolved out of the eastern variant of Northern Brahmi (Late Gupta) during the 8th century CE. By the 18th century, Nargari had fully evolved into Devanagari, to become the principal script of northern India.

The term Nagari is derived from the Sanskrit word 'nagar' meaning 'urban', 'city'or 'metropolitan script.' Nagari was the dominant script form in the Middle Ages, used to write Sanskrit between 1000 and 1200 AD, replacing the Siddham script. Between the 14th and 18th century the script developed nearer to its present day Devanagari form.

Nagari was used in central and southwest India and produced regional variants. The Nandinagari script was used in southern India between the 8th and 19th centuries to write Sanskrit inscriptions and texts in southern Mararashtra, Karnataka and Andra Pradesh. Archaic forms of Nandinagari are dated back as far as the 6th and 7th centuries. But its form was firmly established by 10th century. Nandinagari has never been used for printing, hence it lacks refinement and standardization. The meaning of its name is obscure but it maybe related to its locality or the worship of Shiva.

A script of capital letters, Nagari is traditionally written from left to right, using a square cut nibbed pen dipped in Indian ink onto prepared birch bark, which allows for the marking of straight lines. This enabled scribes to create the defining calligraphic feature of Nagari script, the vertical bar and horizontal bar that help form the letter. Nagari has the headline stroke at the top of individual letters, but lacks the long connecting line that groups letters into words. The later extentended horizontal line came to define the Devanagari script.

Devanagari

Devanagari has been the official script of India since 1944. Employed to write the Indo-Aryan language of Sanskrit and its Prakrits – Hindi, Marathi, Nepali, Gujarati, Bhilli, Bhojpuri, Konkani, Magdhi, Maithilli, Mawari, Newari, Pahari, Santhali, Thoru and sometimes Sindhi, Punjabi and Kashmiri. Hindi is the most spoken language in India and fourth in the world.

The name Devanagri is made up of two Sanskrit words 'Deva' which means god, brahmin or celestial, and 'Nagari' meaning urban, metropolitan or city. In English this can be translated two ways, "heavenly/sacred script of the city" or "script of the city of the Gods or priests". It has been known by this name since the 11th century AD, due to its ubiquitous use for writing Sanskrit. At the beginning of the 21st century, it is commonly called by its nickname 'Deva lipi' or godly, holy, sacred script.

Devanagari began life as a revised Nagari script called Balabadha. It was revised during the middle ages to write Dravidian, Tibetan and Burman and became called Darivardhita or southern script. Some Devanagari letters come in two calligraphic forms. The Mumbai variant used in southern India has become the standardised, classic form. The Kulkota variant is the northern, modern form, revered as the magical form of Devanagari by western Tantrics. Devanagari is the parent of three 15th century variant scripts; Kaithi – used by the Kayasth caste of writers and clerics, Gujarati – a merchant script with no horizontal bar, and Modi – a cursive script for writing Marithi.

Horizontal and Vertical Bars

The horizontal bar is thought to be a development from the nail-headed scripts of central India, it become an integral and essential feature of Nagari script. Originally, the horizontal line was limited to the individual letter and did not join the next letter. The continuous horizontal line is a later development and differentiates the earlier Nagari script from the later Devanagari script. The continuous horizontal line gives the letters the appearance of hanging from a line. The line is only broken between words with a final vowel, diphthong, nasal (anusvara) or weak aspirant (visarga) and words with an initial consonant. Rather than writing a succession of individual words, Sanskrit orthography is sensitive to breath groups representing connected discourse.

The vertical bar is an essential part of Nagari script. In earlier Brahmi scripts the vertical bar is absent, it shows in the addition of the 'aa' matra to a consonant, so that it could be fully pronounced and written. In some letters, the vertical bar is short and goes on the top of forms, because a full line cannot be drawn through. The vertical line is cancelled by a halant sign in the case of letters used to represent the half pronounced phoneme. These half signs also help to form conjunct letters. The suggestion to make half letters from full letters by adding a halant sign has been helpful for pronunciation. After the vertical bar is drawn predominantly the graphics becomes 'Devi-Lipi'.

Ganypata

Ganypata is another name for the elephant headed God Ganesha. He was given it when he was chosen by Shiva to be 'lord or leader of the ganas', Shiva's attendants. According to the tradition of the scribes of the Ganapati School, one scribe came to write copies of the Mahabharata for the author Vyasa Muni. Ganesha introduced the vertibar of 'A' vowel. This feature is high-lighted by Vyasa in Bhagwad Gita wherein Krishna says, "I am the common factor of Aa kaar in all letters." Thus this feature was added in all consonantal designs. All consonant designs either touch or cross the vertical bar. There are exceptions in the designs of the letters Ga, Na, Sha. These letters do not touch the vertical bar. This graphic peculiarity points to the fact that writing is a Ganesh Vidya.

अ आ इ ई उ ऊ ऋ ॠ लृ लॄ ए ऐ ओ औ अं अः

2 lines of Nagari

पढकर मुझे ज्ञात हुआ कि आप मेरी
हूँ, मुझे भी घर की बहुत याद आ रही

2 lines of Devanagari

a	aa	i	ii	u	uu	ri	lri	e	ai	o	au

ka	kha	ga	gha	nga	ca	cha	ja	jha	nya	tta	thha	dda	dhha	nna	ta	tha	da

dha	na	pa	pha	ba	bha	ma	ya	ra	la	va	sha	ssha	sa	ha

Nandinagari

अ आ इ ई उ ऊ ऋ ॠ लृ लॄ ए ऐ ओ औ अं अः

a	aa	i	ii	u	uu	ri	rii	lri	lrii	e	ai	o	au	am	ah

क ख ग घ ङ च छ ज झ ञ ट ठ ड ढ ण

ka	kha	ga	gha	nga	ca	cha	ja	jha	nya	tta	ttha	dda	ddha	nna

त थ द ध न प फ ब भ म य र ल व श ष स ह

ta	tha	da	dha	na	pa	pha	ba	bha	ma	ya	ra	la	va	sha	ssha	sa	ha

Southern Devanagari (standard / classic)

a	aa	i	ii	u	uu	ri	rii	lri	lrii	e	ai	o	au	am	ah

ka	kha	ga	gha	nga	ca	cha	ja	jha	nya	tta	ttha	dda	ddha	nna

त थ द ध न प फ ब भ म य र ल व श ष स ह

ta	tha	da	dha	na	pa	pha	ba	bha	ma	ya	ra	la	va	sha	ssha	sa	ha

Northern Devanagari (modern)

a	aa	li	lii	o	au

am	ah	kha	jha	nna	la

Northern variants

ga	nna	sha

Ganesh Vidya.

Devanagari

In northern India, the Late Gupta Brahmi script evolved the Nagari script around 1000 CE. By the 14th century, Nagari had become the Devanagari script. In the 15th century the Devanagari script inspired three related cursive scripts, in northern and central India.

Kaithili

Kaithili is a Nagari derived script from the 14th century used to write Bhojpuri, Magdha, Urdu, Awadhi, Maithili and Bengali. A historical script used predominately in the northern states of Bihar and Uttar Pradesh, most widely used in the provinces of Awadh, Bhojpur and Madesh in Nepal, for writing legal, administrative and private records in princely courts and colonial governments.

A cursive form of Devanagari generally written without a headline or matra but with serifs, especially in printing. Although Kaithili was more widely used in north India than Devanagari in some areas, it later lost its popularity to other officially recognized scripts.

During the British colonial period the use of Kaithi was discouraged, except in Bihar, where it was made the official script of government offices and courts. As a result it is also known as the Bihar script. Elsewhere it was mainly used by the Kayastha, a Brahmin caste made up mostly of scribes and clerks, and the name Kaithi is derived from Kayastha, which means 'scribe' in Sanskrit, referring to the "lower classes" to whom an education in Devanagari was considered an unnecessary luxury.

Kaithi was widely used until the early 20th century, since then it has been largely replaced by Devanagari or other scripts, although it is apparently used to some extent in personal correspondence in rural areas.

Gujarati

Gujurati is a Indo-Aryan language spoken in Gujarat, Maharashtra, Rajasthan, Karnataka, and Madhya Pradesh. The Gujarati script was adapted from the Devanagari script to write the Gujarati language with the earliest known documents dating from 1592 and first used in print in a 1797 advertisement. A merchant script with no horizontal bar, until the 19th century it was mainly used for writing letters and keeping accounts, while the Devanagari script was used for literature and academic writings.

Modi (Marathi)

Modi is a cursive script invented in the 17th century to write the Indo-Aryan Marathi language, spoken in the state of Maharashatra. Frequently used as a shorthand script in business and administration, it has also been used to write Urdu, Kannada, Gurjarti, Rajasthani, Hindi and Tamil.

The Marathi word Modi means "to bend or break." Believed to be derived from a Devanagari variant called Balbooth used for continuous writing. The Modi letters are considered to be "broken" versions of these characters. Devanagari replaced Modi for writing Marathi in 1950.

श्र श्रा २ ई उ ऊ ए ऐ श्रो श्रौ

| a | aa | i | ii | u | uu | e | ai | o | au |

क ખ ग ઘ ઙ य छ ण ह ञ

| ka | kha | ga | gha | na | ca | cha | ja | jha | na |

ट ડ ઙ ड ઢ ढ म ण थ द य ण

| ta | tha | da | ddha | dha | rha | na | tta | ttha | dda | ddha | na |

प स्थ व भ म य र ल व द श ष स ह

| pa | pha | ba | bha | ma | ya | ra | la | va | sa | sa | sa | ha |

Kaithili

અ આ ઇ ઈ ઉ ઊ ઋ એ ઐ ઓ ઔ અં અઃ

| a | aa | i | ii | u | uu | ru | e | ai | o | au | am | ah |

ક ખ ગ ઘ ઙ ચ છ જ ઝ ઞ

| ka | kha | ga | gha | na | ca | cha | ja | jha | na |

ટ ઠ ડ ઢ ણ ત થ દ ધ ન પ ફ બ ભ મ

| tta | ttha | dda | ddha | na | ta | tha | da | dha | na | pa | pha | ba | bha | ma |

ય ર લ વ શ ષ સ હ ળ ક્ષ જ્ઞ

| ya | ra | la | va | sa | sa | sa | ha | la | ksa | jna |

Gujarati

अ आ ई उ ए ऐ ओ औ

| a | aa | i | u | e | ai | o | au |

क ह ग घ ङ च छ ण झ ञ

| ka | kha | ga | gha | na | ca | cha | ja | jha | na |

ट ठ ड ढ ण त छ द ध न

| tta | ttha | dda | ddha | na | ta | tha | da | dha | na |

प प छ म म व य र ल व श ष स ह ळ

| pa | pha | ba | bha | ma | ya | ra | la | va | sa | sa | sa | ha | la |

Modi

Bangla

The northeast region of the Indian subcontinent stretches from Bengal to the Burmese border and includes the nation of Bangladesh (East Bengal) and the states of West Bengal, Assam, Orissa, Arunachal Pradesh, Nagaland, Manipur, Mizoram, Tripura and Meghalaya. The dominant script of this region is Bangla lipi or Bengali script, the sixth most used writing system in the world.

Employed to write Bengali and Assamese, with minor alterations, in Bangladesh, West Bengal, Assam, Tripura, the Andaman and Nicobar islands. It is also the basis for other writing systems like Maithili, Bhojpuri, Manipuri, Mizo, Naga, Santalli, and Sanskrit. During the first millennium CE, Bengal (Kolkata) was a hub of Sanskrit literature.

Sometimes called Eastern Nagari or Eastern Neo-Brahmic, Bangla evolved from the Late Gupta script around 1000 CE. The Nagari script style is defined by hanging letters from a visible headline or matra. This was made possible by the use of writing with a square cut nibbed pen on prepared tree bark which allowed for the use of straight lines.

Originally Bangla was not associated with any particular language but was often used in the middle kingdoms of India and in the Pala empire. Its proto form for writing Bengali and Assamese was called Gaudi. Later, it continued to be used specifically in the Bengal region and came to be called Bangla meaning Bengali.

Standardised into its modern form by Iswar Chanda, under the reign of the East India Company. The current printed form first appeared in 1778 when Charles Wilkins developed printing in Bengali with a few archaic letters modernized in the 19th century. Today it is the official script of Bangladesh, although Muslim, they still speak Bengali.

Bengali

The second most spoken language in India and seventh in the world, Bengali is an eastern Indo-Aryan language closely related to Sanskrit, spoken in the Indian states of West Bengal, Assam and Bangladesh (East Bengal). A dialect of Magdhi Prakrit, it evolved as a distinct regional language between 1000-1200 CE which in turn evolved into three groups, Bengal/Assamese, Bihari, and Odia languages. The Bengali version of Bangla lipi used to write Bengali, differs slightly from Assamese and Maithili Bangla.

Assamese

Assamese is an Indo-Aryan language related to Bengali and Odia. It is spoken in the states of Assam, Meghalaya, Arunachal Pradesh, Bangladesh and Bhutan. The Assamese developed their Bangla alphabet around 1200 CE and it closely resembles the Bengali and Maithili alphabets. In the 18th and 19th centuries, Assamese script divided into three varieties, Kaithili, used by non-brahmins, Barmuniya used by brahmins for Sanskrit, and Gorhgaya used by state officials of the Ahom kingdom.

Maithili

Maithili is a Bihari language of the east Indic group of Indo-Aryan languages with official status, spoken in the east Indian state of Bihar and eastern Nepal. The Maithili language was formally written in a variety of Bangla script called Milthilaksara or Tirauta. Maithili has also been written in the Kaithi script, a script used to translate other neighbouring languages such as Bhojpuri, Magdhi and Awadi. But these days is normally written in the Devanagari script.

graphic variation of the initial letter A in eastern India

a	aa	i	u	uu	e	ai	o	au

ka	kha	ga	gha	na	ca	cha	ja	jha	na	tta	ttha	dda	ddha	na

ta	tha	da	dha	na	pa	pha	ba	bha	ma	ya	ra	la	sa	sa	sa	ha	khya

proto Bengali

a	aa	i	ii	u	e	ai	o

ka	kha	ga	gha	na	tha	ttha	dta	na	tta	ttha	dda	ddha	na

ta	tha	da	dha	na	pa	ba	bha	na	ja	ra	la	ra	sa	sa	sa	ha

proto Assamese

Gaudi / proto Bangla

a	aa	i	ii	u	uu	ri	e	ai	o	au

ka	kha	ga	gha	na	ca	cha	ja	jha	na	tta	ttha	dda	ddha	na	ta	tha

da	dha	na	pa	pha	ba	bha	ma	ya	ra	la	sa	sa	sa	ha	ya	a	ha

Bangla / Bengali

a	aa	i	ii	u	uu	e	ai	o	au	khya

vowel variants of the Tirhuta / Mithilakshar / Maithili script   Assames consonant

Bangla

As the dominant script of northeast India, Bangla lipi has had its alphabet order adapted to write other Indo-Aryan and Tai Kidai languages, spoken from West Bengal to the Burmese border. This includes the nation of Bangladesh (East Bengal) and the Indian states of Assam, Orissa, Arunachal Pradesh, Nagaland, Manipur, Mizoram, Tripura and Meghalaya.

Oriya

Oriya is an Indo-Aryan language spoken mainly in the state of Orissa and west Bengal. It is closely related to Assamese and Bengali, and is also used to write Sanskrit. The Oriya script developed from an early southern Brahmi variant called Kalinga, around 1000 AD. The modern Oriya style is a hybrid script, its inner, alphabetic form bearing a close resemblance to Bengali. Its curvilinear outer form is reminiscent of southern Indian scripts, a feature attributed to the fact that it was initially written on palm leaves with a pointed stylus. The vertical bar characteristic of Nagari and Bengali has been transformed into a semi circle which appears at the top of most letters.

Sylheti Nagri

Considered to be a dialect of Bengali, Sylheti (English) or Syloti is an east Indo-Aryan language spoken in Bangladesh and Assam. Sylheti Nagri is the original script used to write the Sylheti language but has been almost entirely replaced by Bengali. The script differs from Bangla as it is a form of Kaithi script used in the state of Bihar. At its peak it was used by nearly all literate Sylheti speakers for personal correspondence, record keeping, business purposes and religious texts in the language. Legend has it the Saint Shahjalal, who converted to Islam during the 14th century, devised the script, as other scripts in use at the time were deemed unsuitable

The earliest manuscripts date from the 17th century, but by the end of the 17th century, the Delhi Sulanate declared Persian to be the official language of the region and the Perso-Arabic, Nasta-liq script was used in all official documents, although Sylheti Nagri continued to be used informally. The first Sylheti printing press was established in 1870 and literacy in the script became high but the script went into decline after the partition of India in 1947, and by 1970 had fallen almost entirely out of use, mainly employed by linguists and academics.

Manipuri

Manipuri is one of the official languages of the northeast state of Manipur. It is a member of the Tibeto-Burmese branch of the Sino-Tibetan language family and is also spoken in Bangladesh and Myanmar.

The origins of the Manipuri script are obscure as many historical documents were destroyed in the 18th century. Some believe the script has been used for almost 4000 years, while others think it developed from the Bengali script during in the 17th century. Between the 17th and 20th century, the Manipuri language was written in the Bengali script. In the mid 20th century, Manipuri scholars campaigned to replace Bengali script with a scholarly reconstruction of the ancient Manipuri script. Since the mid 1980s, the Manipuri language has been written in schools.

Chakma

The Chakma language is an east Indian language closely related to Bengali, spoken in Bangladesh, Mizoram, Assam and Tripuri. It is written in a cursive Brahmi derived script called Chakma Ajhapau, similar to that of the Mon or Burmese script. It is also spelt Ojhapath, Ojhopath or Aaojhapath.

Ahom

Ahom or Tai Ahom is a Tai-Kadai language formerly spoken in the Indian state of Assam, where the Ahom people, who originally came from Yunnan province in China, ruled the Brahmaputra valley between 1228 to 1826. Ahom was used as the sole language of the Ahom kingdom until the 15th or 16th century, when it started to be replaced by Assamese. Derived from the Brahmi script, the earliest inscriptions, on a stone pillar, dates from the 15th century. The alphabet also appears on coins, brass plates and numerous manuscripts on cloth or bark.

By the early 19th century Ahom was no longer used as a spoken language, although it continued to be used in religious ceremonies throughout the 19th century. Since 1920 efforts have been made to revive the Ahom language and culture.

ଅ ଆ ଇ ଈ ଉ ଊ ର ରୂ ଌ ୡ ଏ ଐ ଓ ଔ

a · aa · i · ii · u · uu · ri · rii · li · lii · e · ai · o · au

କ ଖ ଗ ଘ ଙ ଚ ଛ ଜ ଝ ଞ ଟ ଠ ଡ ଢ ଣ

ka · kha · ga · gha · na · ca · cha · ja · jha · na · tta · ttha · dda · ddha · na

ତ ଥ ଦ ଧ ନ ପ ଫ ବ ଭ ମ ଯ ୟ ର ଲ ଳ ଶ ଷ ସ ହ

ta · tha · da · dha · na · pa · pha · ba · bha · ma · ya · ya · ra · la · la · sa · sa · sa · ha

Oriya

a · aa · i · u · e · o · ko · kho · go · gho · co · cho · jo · jho · to · tho · do · dho

to · tho · do · dho · no · po · pho · bo · bho · mo · ro · lo · ro · so · ro

Sylheti Nagri

ka · kha · ga · gha · na · ca · cha · ja · jha · na · ta · tha · da · dha · na · ta · tha

da · dha · na · pa · pha · ba · bha · ma · ya · ra · la · va · sa · sa · sa · ha · ksa · a

Old Manipuri

k · kh · pa · ph · t · th · g · gh · b · bh · d · dh · dj · djh

c · u · n · l · m · n · w · s · j · h · r · a

Manipuri

aa · i · u · e · ka · kha · ga · gha · na · ca · cha · ja · jha · na · tta · ttha · dddha · dha

na · ta · tha · da · dha · na · pa · pha · ba · bha · ma · yya · ya · ra · la · wa · sa · ha

Chakma

(a) · ka · kha · nga · na · ta · pa · pha · ba · ma · ja · cha · tha

ra · la · sa · nya · ha · da · ga · gha · jha · dha · bha

Ahom script

Nepalese Mol

Mol is a Nepalese word meaning 'head' used as a classification for seven Brahmi derived scripts that help to make up 'Nepali lipi' or the family of Nepalese scripts. Traditionally, Nepali lipi is the name given to all the major scripts of Nepal. These scripts are used to write the Indo-Aryan Nepali, and the Tibeto-Burman, Nepal Bhasa or Newari languages. These two Nepalese languages have been written in nine different national scripts – Bhujinmol, Golmol, Hinmol, Kwenmol, Kunmol, Litumol, Pachumol, Prachalit and Ranjana – all of which are classified as Nepali lipi.

The most popular and widely used of these is called Ranjana, also called Kutila or Nepali lipi in Nepal, and Lantsa in Tibet. Ranjana is the most widely used form of Nepali lipi to write the Nepal Bhasa/Newari language. It is a 10th century Devanagari derived script, whereas the other eight are thought to have evolved from a primary script developed during the 8th century, from the Kutila form of the eastern Late Gupta Brahmi script variant.

All these scripts were still in widespread use between the 19th century and the early 20th century, when they went into decline. In 1906, the Rana regime supplanted the use of Nepali lipi with Devanagari, possible due to the availability of moveable type for printing.

Since the fall of the Rana regime in 1951, efforts have been made to revive the old scripts. Although they are still not in general use, they are used as display lettering for signage, invitation and greetings cards, letterheads, book and CD covers, product labels and newspaper mastheads. In the eastern border regions of Nepal and Sikkim, the related Lepcha and Limbu script are used for writing Nepal Bhasa.

Kutila

Nepali lipi are considered to be of the Kutila calligraphic style. The term, 'kutil' means 'crooked' or 'bent'. The term refers to the right angled down stroke created by a sharp twist of the pen at the end of a letter vertical downstroke. It first appeared as a calligraphic style in conjunction with the Late Gupta Brahmi script, and is found in both Devanagari and Bangla calligraphy.

Mol (Bhujinmol, Golmol, Hinmol, Kwenmol, Kunmol, Litumol, Pachumol)

Used to write Sanskrit, Nepali and Nepal Bhasa/Newari, Mol are mainly thought to be derived from the Bangla script of northeast India. They may be considered as seven of the nine documented script styles of Nepali lipi – Bhujinmol, Golmol, Hinmol, Kwenmol, Kunmol, Litumol and Pachumol – are the oldest forms of Nepali lipi. The other two being Prachalit, a variant of Mol, and Ranjana, also called Kutila, a Devanagari variant.

All seven of the stylistic Mol variants are structurally and graphically related. They are distinguished by the shape of their head strokes and named according to the Newari terms for these shapes, with all the names ending in mol meaning 'head'. The oldest of the seven is called Bhujimol meaning 'fly headed' referring to its rounded shape, topped by a headline. Pachumol means 'flat headed'.

Prachalit (Newa/Newar)

Prachalit meaning ordinary, popular, is primarily used for writing the Tibeto-Burman language of Nepal Bhasa or Newari spoken in Nepal, Sikkim and Bhutan. Also called Nepalakshar, Newah Akhah, it is one of the nine scripts classified as Nepali lipi. Derived from Mol script it was used for religious, political and cultural writings. It is still in use as a typeface, published in the Newari edition of the Sikkim Herald.

Kotila (Devanagari)

a	aa	i	ee	u	oo	ri	ree	e	ai	o	au	am	ah

ka	kha	ga	gha	na	cha	chha	ja	jha	yan	ta	tha	da	dha	na	tta	ttha	dda	ddha	na

pa	pha	ba	bha	ma	ya	ra	la	wa	sha	sha	sa	ha	ksha

Bhujimmol

a	aa	i	ee	u	oo	e	ai	o	au

ka	kha	ga	gha	na	cha	chha	ja	jha	yan	ta	tha	da	dha	na	ta	tha	da	dha	na

pa	pha	ba	bha	ma	ya	ra	la	wa	sha	sha	sa	ha	ksha	tra	jna

Golmol

a	aa	i	ee	u	oo	ri	ree	e	ai	o	au	am	ah

ka	kha	ga	gha	na	cha	chha	ja	jha	yan	ta	tha	da	dha	na	ta	tha	da	dha	na

pa	pha	ba	bha	ma	ya	ra	la	wa	sha	sha	sa	ha	ksha	tra	jna

Hinmol

a aa i ee u oo e ai o au

ka kha ga gha na cha chha ja jha yan ta tha da dha na ta tha da dha na

pa pha ba bha ma ya ra la wa sha sha sa ha ksha tra jna

Kunmol

a aa i ee u oo ri ree lri lree e ai o au am ah

ka kha ga gha na cha chha ja jha yan ta tha da dha na ta tha da dha na

pa pha ba bha ma ya ra la wa sha sha sa ha ksha

Kwenmol

a aa i ee u oo ri ree lri lree e ai o au am ah

ka kha ga gha na cha chha ja jha yan ta tha da dha na ta tha da dha na

pa pha ba bha ma ya ra la wa sha sha sa ha ksha tra jna

Litumol

Pacumol

Prachalit

7 styles of Mol

Ranjana

Revered as a sacred script, Ranjana is commonly used by Buddhists monks for writing the Sanskrit titles of books, which have been translated from Sanskrit. It is also employed for inscribing On Mani Padme Hum and other mantras on prayer wheels, shrines, temples and monasteries. Ranjana is also written using a method called Kutaksara (heaped syllables), in which the script is written vertically in columns, instead of horizontally in lines, to form mystical monograms.

Originating in northeast India during the 10th century, Ranjana was used for writing Sanskrit texts and mantras during the Pala dynasty of northeast India, under whose reign Indian Buddhism flourished for the last time. The script spread to Magdha and then to Nepal and Tibet. Under the influence of Tibetan monks it was used for Buddhist inscriptions in China and Japan, as early as the 13th century.

In Nepal, the script is called Ranjana, Kutila or Nepali lipi. In Tibet, the script became known as Lantsa. Tibetan monks also produced a closely related script called Vartu. Both Ranjana and Vartu were used by the Newari people of Nepal. Ranjana being the most widely used script to write the Nepal Bhasa/Newari language. Vartu was in full use for newspapers print until the mid 20th century. It is still used for newspaper headlines.

In medieval Nepal, the script was quickly replaced by other scripts, (Prachalit, Devanagari) but underwent a renaissance in the 16th century. This may have been due to its calligraphic nature, because of its preferred use for ornamental inscriptions of mantras and bijas written in gold with a red outline. This is the main function of Ranjana in Nepal and Tibet, where it is the only Indian script that is still used to some extent.

Ranjana/Kutila

Derived from Late Gupta Brahmi during the 10th century, with the angular or squarish appearance of Nagari script. Ranjana meaning pleasant, delightful, is considered the world's second most beautiful and artistic script. It is composed of thick and thin lines, a thick lined script can mark the paper for a longer duration.

Its characteristic features are, one horizontal line that begins as a fine point then broadens out, and a very fine downstroke at the lower end of the letters that points downwards and to the right, created by means of a quick rotation of the quill at the end of a broad vertical stroke. This stroke defines it as a Kutila calligraphic script. Kutila meaning bent or crooked, referring to the sharp right-angled finishing stroke at the bottom of a thick vertical stroke of a letter.

Lantsa, Vartu

Lantsa (Tib – pleasant, delightful) is the Tibetan version of Ranjana. In the monasteries of Tibet, Lantsa serves as a sacred script used as decoration on murals, printed or signed on mandalas, and the chosen script to write mantras under the title of a Sadhana, which has been translated from Sanskrit into Tibetan. The Vartu or Wartu script (vartula, round) appears to be a more casual form of a handwritten calligraphy. But the basic principles in forms and calligraphy of the consonants are the same as in Lantsa.

Lantsa and Vartu are two Dakini scripts styles which became the fundamental vehicle of Buddhist textual tradition in Nepal and Tibet. From the 8th century CE, in Buddhism, a "terma" represents a form of hidden teaching. If the concealed or encoded teaching or object is a text, it was often written in a 'Dakini' script. In Tibetan Buddhism, Dakini meaning "sky walker" is a female spirit associated with the transmission of teachings to her disciples. Therefore, Dakini is a term used to describe the Brahmi scripts styles employed by Buddhist monks during the 11th century CE for making new copies of the Sutras in Sanskrit.

Tibetan text pages known as "pecha", according to Tibetan tradition, are written by hand or printed from wood-blocks. The text on the front page will have up to 4 lines written in a fancier style than the normal pages. The first line, – the title in Sanskrit, is in Lantsa script, in black ink. In the second line, the same Sanskrit text will be rendered in Vartu script, also in black ink. The third line will be in a Tibetan script, usually in the Uchen style, in red ink. In the last line, the Tibetan translation of the Sanskrit text, written in a Naga or Monastic script, appears in black ink.

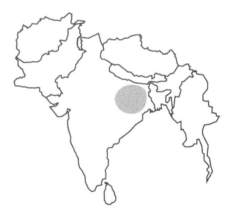

Pala kingdom

| a | aa | i | ii | u | uu | ri | rii | e | o | ai | au | am | ah |

| ka | kha | ga | gha | na | ca | cha | ja | jha | ne | ta | tha | da | dha | na |

| ta | tha | da | dha | na | pa | pha | ba | bha | ma | ya | ra | la | va | sa | sa | sa | ha |

Ranjana / Kutilla

| a | aa | i | ii | u | uu | e | ai | o | au | ri | ree | li | lee | am | ah |

| ka | kha | ga | gha | nga | ca | cha | ja | jha | nya | tta | ttha | dda | ddha | na | ta | tha |

| da | dha | nna | pa | pha | ba | bha | ma | ya | ra | la | va | sa | sha | shha | ha | ksa |

Lantsa

| a | aa | i | ii | u | uu | e | ai | o | au | ri | ree | li | lee | am | ah |

| ka | kha | ga | gha | nga | ca | cha | ja | jha | nya | tta | ttha | dda | ddha | na | ta | tha |

| da | dha | nna | pa | pha | ba | bha | ma | ya | ra | la | va | shha | sha | sa | ha | kssa |

Vartu / Wartu

| ka | kaa | ki | kii | ku | kuu | kri | krii | ke | ko | kai | kau | kam | kah |

Ranjana matra (modifying vowel signs)

Kutaksara

In Tibet, Buddhist monks developed a method for writing syllables in stacks to create complex syllables. They used this technique to compress mantras and form mystical monograms. They chose a specific script to perform this technique which they called Lantsa, the Tibetan equivalent of the Indian word Ranjana, meaning pleasant, delightful.

Ranjana script originated in northeast India in the 10th century. Its letterforms are derived from the Kutila form of Late Gupta with the angular or squarish appearance of Nagari script. It was used during the Pala dynasty of northeast India, under whose reign Indian Buddhism flourished for the last time. Since Ranjana was one of the scripts used for writing Buddhist manuscripts, it accompanied Hindu and Buddhist Tantric texts to Nepal and Tibet.

The script spread to Magdha, then to Nepal where it is still called Kutila, meaning bent or crooked, referring to the sharp right-angled finishing stroke at the bottom of a thick vertical stroke of a letter. In Tibet, the script became known as Lantsa, (Tib – pleasant, delightful).

Ranjana is a revered script, commonly used by Buddhists monks for writing Sanskrit sutras and mantras. Usually the Sanskrit titles of books which have been translated from Sanskrit. Also inscribing On Mani Padme Hum and other mantras on prayer wheels, shrines, temples and monasteries.

In Tibet, the Lantsa letters serve as the basis for a kind of monogram script for devas and mantras. This script form is referred to as Kutaksyar or Kutaksara, meaning 'heaped syllables'. In this script, syllables are superimposed upon each other in such a way that the essential characteristics of the individual letters remain by and large in tact, but coalesce into a single syllable on the model of ligatures used in Brahmi script, without dropping the vowels of the original syllables. Such complex figures can only be deciphered by the specialist or the initiate that may have helped in their development, since they serve as a kind of shorthand for mantras.

The best known example is the mantra of Kalachakra – the powerful ten in Tibetan. It contains in compressed form the seven bija, Ha, Ksa, Ma, La, Ra, Yam, and the three parts of the nasalization sign. Other forms of Kutasksara include the seven letter monogram Ya, Ra, Va, La, Ma , Ksa, Ha, the Heart Sutra and the Lakshmi monogram

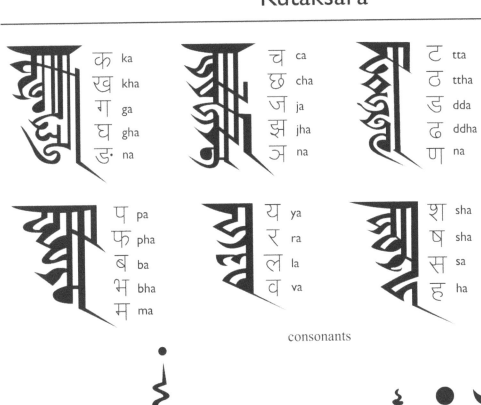

consonants

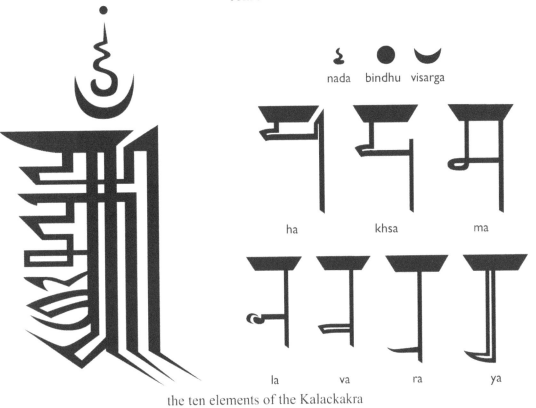

nada   bindhu   visarga

ha   khsa   ma

la   va   ra   ya

the ten elements of the Kalackakra

7 letter monogram

Siddham

Lantsa

Uchen

monogram of Laksmi

Lantsa (woodblock print)

Tibetan Uchen and Ume

The Tibetan alphabet is used to write Tibetan, Dzongka, Sikkimese, Ladakhi and Balti, in Tibet, Nepal, Bhutan and India. It is ancestral to the Limbu and Lepcha alphabets and the multilingual Phags Pa script. The calligraphic excellence and diversity of the divine scripts created by Tibetan Buddhist monks stand shoulder to shoulder with the best from around the world.

The Tibetan national script style was created in the 7th century AD by Thonmi Sombhata, a minister of the first Tibetan Emperor, Songtsen Gompo (569-649 AD). Sombhata was sent to India by the Emperor to study the art of writing. On his return, he introduced his Tibetan script, whose letterforms were based on an Indic alphabet of that period, probably an eastern form of the Gupta-Siddham script.

Gompo created three scripts for writing Tibetan. Uchen – a formal script and typeface. Ume – an informal cursive script for day to day writing. Horyig – a version of the Mongolian square script called Phags Pa. While Uchen may be used to write entire Sutras or Buddhist texts, the rest are more frequently used to write a single phrase or saying.

Uchen

The most common form of formal script used for writing the Tibetan language, Uchen or 'dbu-can' means 'with a head', as it is derived from northern Brahmi origins. As a script it is characterized by its Nagari style, heavy horizontal lines and tapering vertical lines. When hand written, it is the most basic form of Tibetan calligraphy and must be mastered before moving on to other styles. Because of its exceptional clarity, it became the model for letterpress and digital type, establishing Uchen as the international script of Tibet.

Ume

Ume or Umed (dbu-med) means 'headless', as they lack the Nagari style, heavy horizontal top bar of the Uchen script. There are many varieties of Ume script, all of which are cursive informal scripts, for the day to day writing of religious scripture, commentaries and epics, notes, letters and orders etc.

In the Tibetan language. Petsug (dpe-tshug), is a narrow cursive variant used for religious, epic, story and ritual manuscripts. Drugsta (btu-tsha), a script halfway between Uchen and Ume. It used as a display script for titles, headlines, signboards, logo's and tattoos. Tsungtung (tshug-thung), a shortened, abbreviated form, traditionally used for commentaries. Chuyig (khyug-yig), "fast-letters' a highly abbreviated, fluid, cursive version of Ume script.

a   aa   i   u   e   o

ka   kha   ga   nga   ca   cha   ja   nya   ta   tha   da   na

pa   pha   ba   ma   tsa/tza   tsha/tsa   dza   wa

zha   za   '   ya   ra   la   sha   sa   ha

Uchen (headed) - formal script / typeface

penstrokes used in Uchen script

ka   kha   ga   nga   ca   cha   ja   nya   ta   tha   da   na

pa   pha   ba   ma   tsa/tza   tsha/tsa   dza   wa

zha   za   '   ya   ra   la   sha   sa   ha   ra

Ume (headless) - handwriting

Uchen

High/Honourific Uchen

Petsug - Khamyig

Drutsa

High Drutsa

Ornamental Drutsa

Tsugtang (short style)

Tsugring (long style)

Tsugmakhyug

Khyug yig (cursive script)

Khyug dri (quick/nimble script)

Bon Smar

Vjrayana or Tibetan Buddhism differs from traditional Mahayana Buddhism due to the influence of an earlier shamanistic religion known as the Bon religion. Bon was introduced into the mythical pre-Tibetan kingdom of Zhang Zhung by a Buddha like figure called Tonpa Shenrek Minoche from Kazakstan. He combined various native mystical cultures and elements of Hinduism and Zoroasterism to create Bon. He settled in Zhang Zhung, founding the Bon kingdom (100 BCE to 600 CE), the origin of the Shambala myth (Shangrala), and Bon became the official religion of Zhang Zhung. In the 7th century, Zhang Zhumg was conquered by Songtsen Gompo, the first Tibetan king and assimilated into his empire.

Tonpa's followers, called Bonpo's, claim Tonpa lived 18,000 years ago and that his teaching permeated the entire subcontinent and was, in part, responsible for the development of Vedic religion. They say he invented writing, maybe half a millennia earlier than Uchen script.

Smar

Apart from the national scripts of Tibet – Uchen, Ume and Horyig, Tibetan monks have created an array of scripts for writing and translating Sanskrit to Sino-Tibetan. Some of these scripts pre-date the Tibetan national script, while others are simply liturgical scripts from the medieval era.

Followers of the pre-Buddhistic Bon religion, living in the ancient, semi-mythical kingdom of Zhang Zhung, developed script styles which were revived by Tibetan monasteries, who encouraged translators to develop their own scripts from the past (Smar) and present scripts (Lantsa/Vartu), to write Sanskrit texts in Tibetan.

Bon script is called Smar, pronounced Mar, meaning "divine" or "coming from the sky." In the Bon historical records [Chögyal Namkhai Norbu] the so called "Maryig" (Smar script) of Zhang Zhung was the original Bon writing system. In many libraries of old monasteries in Tibet there are ancient manuscripts handwritten in the script referred to as "smar-tshugs" or "lha babs yi ge" (heaven descended script). From the 11th century, Tibetan monks developed new styles from the Old Bon Maryig, as with the Zhang Zhung script, where the shape of calligraphy seems to be developed during the 11th century AD based on a more ancient form.

Naga scripts

The less common Dakini scripts used in Buddhist pechas, other that Lantsa and Vartu, which were used for writing Sanskrit, are called Naga scripts. From the 8th century, Tibetan monks developed Naga scripts to translate Buddhist 'termas' written in Dakini scripts into Tibetan. In some monasteries and other traditional places, translators developed their own scripts out of the Brahmi scripts similar to Lantsa and Vartu, and used these scripts to transcribe Tibetan written thoughts and commentaries to expand the literature at those Holy places

Zhang Zhung

a	aa	i	u	e

ka	kha	ga	nga	ca	cha	ja	nya	ta	tha	da	na	pa	pha	ba	ma

tsa/tza	tsha/tsa	dza	wa	zha	za	'	ya	ra	la	sha	sa	ha

Zhang Zhung Smar

a	aa	i	u	e

ka	kha	ga	nga	ca	cha	ja	nya	ta	tha	da	na	pa	pha	ba	ma

tsa/tza	tsha/tsa	dza	wa	zha	za	'	ya	ra	la	sha	sa	ha

Bon Smar

a	aa	i	u	e

ka	kha	ga	nga	ca	cha	ja	nya	ta	tha	da	na	pa	pha	ba	ma

tsa/tza	tsha/tsa	dza	wa	zha	za	'	ya	ra	la	sha	sa	ha

a	i	u	e	o	ai	ka	ca	tta	ta	pa	ya	sha

Translator

a	ka	ca	ta	tta	pa	ya	sha

Vajra Monastry

a	ka	ca	tta	ta	pa	ya	sha

Great Old Monk

Naga or Monastic scripts for translating Sanskrit to Tibetan

Bhutan and Sikkim Brahmi

The kindom of Bhutan and the northeastern Indian state of Sikkim are small Himalayan regions situated on either side of Tibet. The Brahmi abugida arrived in Bhutan and Sikkim from Tibet during the 16th century, where it was adapted to write the Tibeto-Burman languages of Nepal Bhasa/Newari, Lepcha, Limbu and Kiratia. They are the only Sino-Tibetan languages in the Central Himalayas to posses their own scripts, others use Devanagari.

Lepcha (Rong)

Lepcha (Rong-Ríng), is a Tibeto-Burman language spoken by about 65,00 people in the Indian states of Sikkim, West Bengal and Kalimpong, also in Nepal and Bhutan. The Lepcha script is derived from the Tibetan script and may have Burmese influences. Early manuscripts in Lepcha are written vertically, a sign of Chinese influence. When they were written horizontally, the letters remained in their new orientation, rotated 90 degrees from their Tibetan prototypes. The changes in writing direction have resulted in a metamorphosis of the eight syllable-final consonants from conjuncts as in Tibetan to superimposed diacritics.

According to Lepcha tradition, the script was invented by the Lepcha scholar, Thikúng Men Salóng sometime during the 17th century. Another theory is that the script developed during the early years of the 18th century, under the patronage of Prince Chakdar Namqyai of the Tibetan dynasty in Sikkim.. Today the Lepcha script is used in newspapers, magazines, textbooks, collections of poetry, prose and plays.

Limbu / Kirat Sirijinga

Limbu, also Yakthungba Pan or Yakthungpan, is a Tibeto-Burman language spoken by about 280,000 people in eastern Nepal, Bhutan and northern India. The word limbu means 'archer.' Historical documentation tells us that the Limbu or Kirat Sirijinga script was devised during a period of Buddhist expansion in Sikkim in the early 18th century, when Limbuwan still consituted part of Sikkim terratory.

Limbu was probably modelled on the Lepcha alphabet, which is thought to have derived from the Tibetan alphabet. According to many historians, King Sirijonga invented the "Kirat-Sirijinga Script" in the late 9th century. It disappeared for many years and was then reintroduced by Te-ongsi Sirijonga (believed to be a reincarnation of King Sirijonga), in the 17th century. In 1925, Iman Singh Chemjong, a Limbu scholar, named the script after the Limbu hero Sirijonga, who had laid down his life for the preservation and promotion of script in 1743.

Kirat Rai

Usually written in Devanagari, Bantawa is a member of the Easter Kiranti branch of Tibeto-Burman languages spoken by an estimated 390,000 Bantawa Rai ethinic group, in parts of Sikkkim and Nepal. In Sikkim, the Rai language is written in a script known as Kirat Rai, a modified version of the Khambu Rai script used to write the same language in Nepal.

It is said that the Khmabu Rai script was originally created by Sirijonga Hay in the 9th century, who adapted the Brahmi system. The script then disappeared form many years until it was re-introduced in the 17th century. The script was developed for purpose in the 1980s by Kripasalyan Rai.

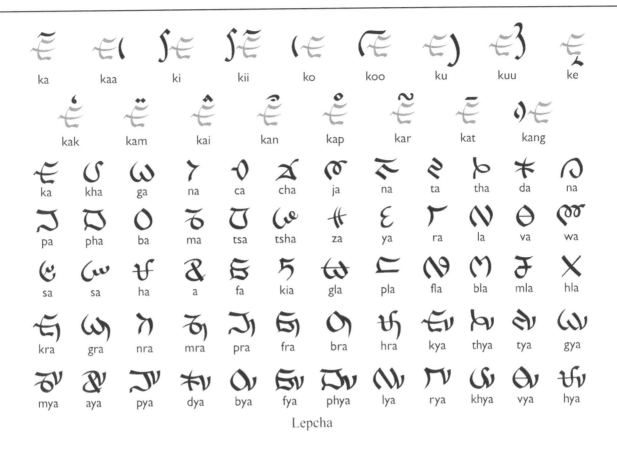

ka · kaa · ki · kii · ko · koo · ku · kuu · ke

kak · kam · kai · kan · kap · kar · kat · kang

ka · kha · ga · na · ca · cha · ja · na · ta · tha · da · na

pa · pha · ba · ma · tsa · tsha · za · ya · ra · la · va · wa

sa · sa · ha · a · fa · kia · gla · pla · fla · bla · mla · hla

kra · gra · nra · mra · pra · fra · bra · hra · kya · thya · tya · gya

mya · aya · pya · dya · bya · fya · phya · lya · rya · khya · vya · hya

Lepcha

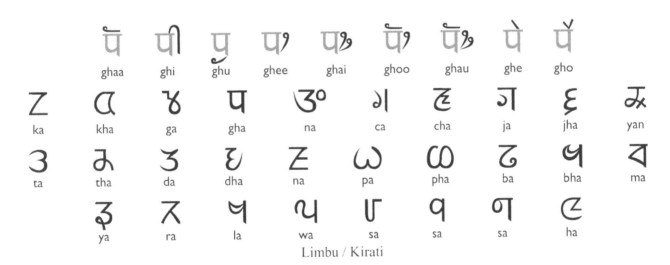

ghaa · ghi · ghu · ghee · ghai · ghoo · ghau · ghe · gho

ka · kha · ga · gha · na · ca · cha · ja · jha · yan

ta · tha · da · dha · na · pa · pha · ba · bha · ma

ya · ra · la · wa · sa · sa · sa · ha

Limbu / Kirati

ka · kaa · ki · ku · ke · kai · ko · kau · k · vowel carrier

ka · kha · ga · gha · na · ca · cha · ja · jha · na · ta · tha · da · dha

ta · tha · da · dha · na · pa · pha · ba · bha · ma · ya · ra · la · va · sha · sa · ha

Kirat Rai

Central Asian Brahmi

With the spread of Buddhism and trade along the Silk Road during the Gupta era, the Brahmi abugida was adapted by the people of Central Asia – Kyrgystan, Kazakhstan, Uyghur Autonomous China and Mongolia, passing into China, Japan and Korea. Other than Sanskrit, Brahmi was used to write the Indo-Iranian languages of Tocharian and Khotan and the Altaic Mongolian language.

Tocharian

Tocharian is an extinct branch of the Indo-Iranian language group, spoken in the Tamarin Basin, now part of Xin Jiang in the Uyghur Autonomous Region of China. The script was in use between the 6th and 8th centuries CE. The language and its script disappeared after the arrival of the Uyghurs, who were expelled from Mongolia by the Kyrgyz.

Khotan

Khotan is a dialect of Saka, an Indo-Iranian language related to Gandhari and Sogdian, spoken in Xin Jiang, China. The Khotanese arrived in the Tamarin Basin from Kyrgystan, when it was a center of study and practise of Mahayana Buddhism with Sanskrit, Prakrit, Tibetan and Chinese spoken there. Khotan was written in a Gupta-Brahmi derived script with a structure similar to Tibetan and influences from Kharosthi. Used until the 10th century, ended by Islamic conquest.

Bhaiksuki

Found exclusively in Buddhist texts with only eleven inscriptions and four manuscripts, Bhaiksuki is an extinct Gupta-Brahmi derived script used between the 11th and 12th centuries in Bihar and Tibet for writing Sanskrit. Also called Sindura and point-headed or arrow-headed script by the English, due to the shape of the letters. Many are capped with one or more arrows due to the use of a thick nibbed pen.

Soyombo

The word Soyombo means "self developed Holy letters." They were derived from the Devanagari script by a Mongolian monk and scholar called Bogdo Zanabazar in 1686 to write Mongolian, Sanskrit and Tibetan on prayer wheels, official seals and temples.

Chinese Cursive

Nepalese, Chinese and Japanesee monks have written Sanskrit in Devanagari using the Chinese cursive script, brush style. Such examples are scarce.

a	aa	i	ii	u	uu	ri	rii	e	ai	o	au	ah

ka	kha	ga	gha	nga	ca	cha	ja	jha	nya	tta	ttha	dda	ddha	na

ta	tha	da	dha	nna	pa	pha	ba	bha	ma	ya	ra	la	wa	shha	sha	sa	ha

Tocharian

a	aa	i	ii	u	uu	e	ai	o	au	ah	ei

ka	kha	ga	gha	nga	ca	cha	ja	jha	nya	tta	ttha	dda	ddha	na

ta	tha	da	dha	nna	pa	pha	ba	bha	ma	ya	ra	rra	la	wa	shha	sha	sa	ha

Khotan

a	aa	i	ii	u	uu	e	ai	o	au	ri	rii	li

ka	kha	ga	gha	nga	ca	cha	ja	jha	nya	tta	ttha	dda	ddha	na

ta	tha	da	dha	nna	pa	pha	ba	bha	ma	ya	ra	la	wa	shha	sha	sa	ha

Bhaiksuki

a	i	u	e	o	aa	ii	uu	ee	oo	ai	au	u	u	o	o

ga	ka	nga	ja	ca	na	da	ta	na	ba	pa	ma	ya	ra	wa	la	sha	sa	ha	kssa

Soyombo

(Devanagari) Chinese Cursive

Square Script

Square script is the name given to a form of Asian calligraphy employed across medieval Mongolia, China and Tibet to write Sanskrit, Mongolian, Chinese and Tibetan. The original form of Square script is called Phags Pa, named after a Tibetan llama called Bio-gros rGyalantshan, who was better known by the title of the Phags Pa llama The script was commissioned in 1250 CE by Kublai Khan, to create a new national script to replace the semitic derived Uigur based script, which was devised in 1208.

In 1259, Kublai issued edicts requiring all official documents to use the new script along with the local script. It is probable that Kublai wanted the script to write all the languages of his empire and ordered the establishment of schools to teach the new script. The Old Mongolian script was of semitic descent and thought to be unsuitable for Mongolian because it was borrowed from the Uigurs, and was even less suitable for Chinese.

The script was originally called "New Mongolian letters" a name still used in Tibet where it is called Horyig. However the script is known as Square script in Mongolia and as Phags Pa letters in Chinese, although it is more commonly referred to as Seal script, as it was used for making seals. In English, it is referred to as Mongolian Quadratic script, or more commonly Phags Pa script, a name with many variant spellings.

The Phags Pa script didn't prove popular with Mongolian and Chinese officials, who only used the new script to a limited extent and reluctantly. Usage of the new script among private individuals was even more limited. All the edicts prohibiting the use of the Old Mongol script had little effect. The Chinese completely abandoned it in 1368, following the collapse of the Yuan dynasty. At the sametime, the Mongols reverted back to their Uigur based script.

The most recent example of Phags Pa script in Mongolian is dated from 1352, though there are later examples in Chinese. However, the script is still used in Tibet for decoration on seals and temple inscriptions. It is also used to write some business names in Mongolian. The script can be written vertically in columns or horizontally in lines.

Mongol Horizontal Square Script is based on the Tibetan, Horyig script. It was invented by Bogdo Zanabazar, first leader of Tibetan Buddhism in Mongolia, who also created the Mongolian, Devanagri variant called Soyomo.

Square Script

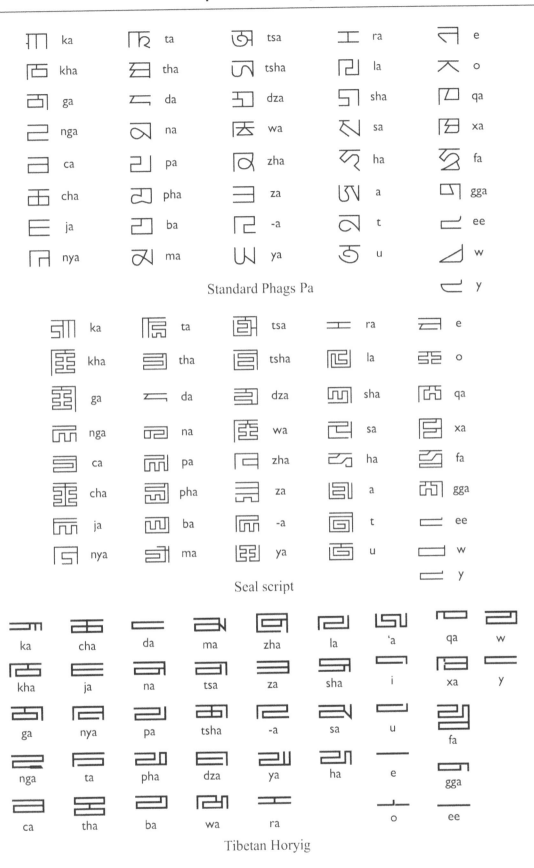

Standard Phags Pa

Seal script

Tibetan Horyig

Mongolian horizontal square script

Southern Brahmi

Brahmi lipi is the parent of several Influential southern variants, including the historically important Grantha scripts. They were used to write Sanskrit and the Dravidian languages of Tamil, Malayalam, Kannada, Tulu and Telugu. They also influenced the scripts of the Indo-Aryan Prakrits of Konkani, Sinhala and Maldivian. From 3rd century CE onwards, these Brahmi variants developed through the dynasties of the Kalingas, Kadambas, Pallavas, Cholas, Chalukyas, Pandyas. Gangas, Rashtrakutas and Vjayangaras to evolve into the modern scripts of southern India.

Early southern variants include the proto-Brahmi scripts of Bhattiprolu and Tamil Brahmi, thought to pre-date Muaryan Brahmi. Early post-Muaryan forms include the Kalinga and Kadamba/Pallava dynastic variants. Between the 6th and 8th centuries CE, the Kadamba/Pallava variant diverged into two separate forms for writing Kannada and Telugu and Tamil. Southern Indian scripts are generally rounded or cursive which comes from the practice of writing with a sharp stylus on palm leaves that tend to split where straight lines are used. Although some are distinguished by the use of long descenders and arched ascenders.

Over the same time period, religion and trade carried the southern Brahmi variants to southeast Asia, from which evolved the national scripts of Burma, Cambodia, Laos, Thailand and Vietnam. They were also carried to Malaysia, Indonesia, Sumatra and the Philippines, where it was adapted to write the native languages before the arrival of the Chinese, Roman and Arabic scripts.

Bhattiprolu

The earliest inscriptions in proto-Brahmi script are found on pieces of pottery dated between 600 and 400 BCE from Tamil Nadu and Sri Lanka. The earliest form of Brahmi to write Dravidian languages comes from the city of Bhattiprolu in Andhra Pradesh, circa 400 BCE. The inscriptions are on an urn containing Buddhist relics written in Pali and Telugu. Of the 23 signs to be identified so far, two correspond to Muaryan Brahmi and two to modern Telugu. These signs reflect a possible connection between pre-existing forms and the later signs of Brahmi. The letters are clearly related to the geometric forms of circle, ellipse, angle, triangle, square, quadrangle.

Tamil-Brahmi

The most ancient non-sanskritized Indian literature is recorded in the Tamil language, written in Tamil-Brahmi which had certainly evolved by 200 BC if not as early as 500 BC. Some scholars think the script is derived from the Indus valley script. Firstly, it differs from Muaryan Brahmi by adding several sounds that do not exist in Prakrit. Secondly, in many inscriptions the inherent vowel has been discarded to represent the consonant alone. This is unique to Bhattiprolu and Tamil-Brahmi among the early Brahmi variants. The script is classified into early Tamil-Brahmi 2nd c. BCE to 1st c. CE, and late Tamil-Brahmi 2nd c. to 4th CE.

Kalinga

An early southern Brahmi variant related to the Kadamba script. Kalinga is the ancient name for the northeastern state of Orissa, and Kalinga script was used to write an ancient form of the Indo-Aryan Oriya language. By the 12th century this script has been abandoned in favour of a southern cursive script form to write a Bengali derived alphabet which became the modern Oriya or Odia script.

Southern Brahmi / Kadamba-Pallava

The southern form of Brahmi script can be first seen in the Kadamba-Pallava variant, employed between the 3rd and 5th centuries CE, in the Kadamba and Pallava kingdoms that equate to the modern states of Karnataka, Tamil Nadu and Andhra Pradesh. By the end of the 5th century the script had divided into similar scripts. During the 7th century, under Pallava patronage, southern Brahmi developed into a more elaborate form with longer strokes called Pallava Grantha.

Kadamba

Stylistically different from other southern Brahmi variants by the 5th century CE. The Kadamba script was used roughly in what is nowadays the modern states of Karnataka and Andhra Pradesh in southern India. By the 10th century CE, the Kadamba variant had evolved into the Old Karanese/Kannada script which, under the patronage of the Kadambas, Chalukkyas, Rastrakutas, Shilaharas, and the Haysoulas would ultimately evolve into the modern Kannada and Telugu scripts.

Pallava Grantha

The Pallavas were a highly influential dynasty who practised Hinduism and supported Buddhism, and ruled over modern Tamil Nadu and Andhra Pradesh from the 3rd to the 9th century. Closely related to Kadamba Brahmi, Pallava Brahmi emerged as a distinct script when it split from its original southern Brahmi variant during the 5th century. By the 6th century the script had developed a more rounded, ornate or decorative style called Pallava Grantha. With the spread of Hinduism, Buddhism and trade from south India's east coast during the Pallava dynasty, this script was taken to SE Asia by priests, monks, scholars and traders, where it became the earliest relic of writing in the region, making it the inspiration for the majority of modern southeast Asia scripts.

| a | u | ka | kha | ga | gha | ca | cha | ja | ta | tha | nya | ta | tha | da | dha |

| nae | pa | pha | ba | bha | ma | ya | ra | la | va | sa | sha | shha | ha |

Bhatiprolu

| a | aa | i | ii | u | uu | e | ee | o | oo |

| k | n | c | ch | t | n | t | n | p | m | y | r | l | v | l | ll | r | n |

Tamil Brahmi

| a | i | e | o | ka | kha | ga | gha | ca | cha | ja | tta | thha | dda | nya |

| ta | tha | da | dha | nae | pa | ba | bha | ma | ya | ra | la | va | sa | ha |

Kalinga

| a | aa | i | ii | u | e | o | ka | kha | ga | gha | na | ca | cha | ja | jha | n'a | tta | thha | dda | dhha | nya |

| ta | tha | da | dha | nae | pa | pha | ba | bha | ma | ya | ra | la | va | shha | sha | sa | ha | la | raa |

Southern Brahmi / Kadamba-Pallava

| a | aa | i | u | e | ka | kha | ga | gha | na | ca | cha | ja | n'a | tta | dhha | nya |

| ta | tha | da | dha | nae | pa | pha | ba | bha | ma | ya | ra | la | va | shha | sha | sa | ha |

Kadamba

| a | aa | i | ii | ai | e | o | u | au | ka | kha | ga | gha | na |

| ca | cha | ja | jha | na | ta | tha | da | dha | ma | ta | tha | da | dha | na |

| pa | pha | ba | bha | ma | ya | ra | la | va | sa | sa | sa | ha |

Pallava Grantha (Monumental)

Southern Brahmi

Grantha is an important historical Brahmi derived script, once used to write Sanskrit throughout greater Tamil Nadu. Grantha is a Sanskrit word that denotes a 'literary work – book, text' and the script used for writing Sanskrit was given the same name. Pallava Grantha is an archaic and ornamental form of southern Brahmi script. It is calligraphically distinct from Old Grantha and Modern Grantha, which were created by the Pallavas at a later date to perform the same task. The southern Indian scripts of Tigalari, Malayalam, Sinhala and Tamil are descended from these later Grantha variants.

From the 3rd c CE, the southern Brahmi variant shows elaboration and consonant forms that appear in the later Pallava. By the 5th century, southern Brahmi variants show many features widespread in Pallava Grantha. In the 7th century, Classic Pallava shows the large vowel 'i' matra overhead and consonant stacking, which occurred if two consonants followed one another without an intermediary vowel, the second consonant is made into a subscript and attached to the first.

Pallava Grantha is a florid and elaborate script, it could have not been in everyday use, as it is seen in rock inscriptions and copperplate engravings. The exemplary features of the Pallava Grantha script are its combining of round and rectangular strokes, adding typographic effects such as notches as heads and space filling tails. This made Pallava Grantha eminently suitable for civic and religious inscriptions, still having a monumental feel, yet more decorative.

In southeast Asia, Pallava Grantha was admired, appreciated and emulated. A Pallava king even ruled Kumbajadesa (modern Cambodia and Vietnam) in the 7th century CE. The earliest texts were in Sanskrit and Pali, but soon local languages adopted forms of the script. It became the parent script of Pyu and Mon of Burma, Khmer of Cambodia, Cham of Vietnam, Lanna, Thai and Lao of Thailand and Laos, and Tai Lue and Tai Viet of Burma, Thailand, Vietnam and South China.

Further East, the Pallava script developed a Javanese variant called Kawi script via Tamil, Sanskrit and Mon scripts during the 8th century CE. Its use spread across southeast Asia to become the parent script of Javanese, Balinese, Batak, Baybayin, Kulitan, Buhid, Hanuno'o, Lontra, Old Sudenese, Rencong, Rejang and Tagbanwa scripts of Java, Bali, Sumatra, Borneo and the Philippines. Before they were all succeeded by the modern Arabic and Roman scripts.

South Indian kingdoms

ka
Pallava Grantha

ka
Old Grantha

ka
Tigalari

ka
Malayalam

Western Grantha

ka
Sinhala

ka
Modern Grantha

Eastern Grantha

ka
Modern Tamil

Grantha variants

ornate Brahmi rock inscription 3rd century CE

Chalukya copperplate engraving 5th century CE

Pallava Grantha rock inscription 7th century CE

Thailand

Malayasia

SE Asian Pallava variants

development of Pallava Grantha

Burmese

Northern Thai (Lanna)

khmer

Thai Siam

Lao

Kawi

SE Asian scripts derived from Pallava Grantha

Kannada and Telugu

By the 3rd c. CE, the more cursive form of southern Brahmi had developed into the Kadamba-Pallava script. Under the patronage of the Kadambas, Chalukyas, Rastrakutas, Shilaharas, and Haysoulas the script would ultimately evolve into the modern Kannada and Telugu scripts, which were standardised at the beginning of the 19th century, under the influence of the printing press and Christian missionary organizations.

Old Karanese

Between the 7th and 13th centuries, Old Karanese was used to write Caranese or Kannada, an official language of the Indian states of Masharashtra, Karnataka, Andhra Pradesh, Tamil Nadu and Orissa. By about 1500, the script had morphed into Kannada and Telugu variants, although they remained virtually identical. The introduction of printing in the early 19th century accentuated some minor distinctions between them, giving rise to two systems.

Kannada

One of the major scripts of southern India. Kannada is descended from the Kadamba-Pallava script through the Old Karanese/Kannada script which, by about 1500 had morphed into Kannada and Telugu scripts.

Kannada script is used to write Kannada or Caranese, an official language of the southern Indian states of Karnataka, Andhra Pradesh, Tamil Nadu and Masharashtra. Also used to write Tulu, a southern Dravidian language mainly spoken in the southern states of Karnataka and Kerala, a Tamil dialect called Sankethi and the Indo-Aryan Konkani language spoken in Goa and Karnataka.

Telugu

Telugu is a Dravidian language spoken by about 75 million people mainly in the southern Indian state of Andrha Pradesh where it is the official language. It is also spoken in its neighbouring states of Karnataka, Tamil Nadu, Orissa, Maharashtra and Chattisgarh, and is one of the 22 languages of India.

The Telugu script is a variant of the Old Karanese/Kannada script and a sister script to the modern Kannada script, being virtually identical. Old Karanese split into two separate alphabets between the 12th and 15th centuries CE.

The earliest known inscriptions containing Telugu words appear on coins that date back to 400 BC. The first inscription entirely in Telugu was made in 575 CE, probably inscribed by Renati Cholas, who started writing royal proclamations in Telugu instead of Sanskrit. Telugu developed as a poetical and literary language in the 11th century CE.

ಅ ಆ ಇ ಉ ಎ
a aa i u e

ಕ ಖ ಗ ಘ ಚ ಛ ಜ ಝ ಞ ಟ ಠ ಡ ಢ ಣ
ka kha ga gha na ca cha ja jha na ta tha da dha na

ತ ಥ ದ ಧ ನ ಪ ಫ ಬ ಭ ಮ ಯ ರ ಲ ವ ಳ
ta tha da dha na pa pha ba bha ma ya ra la va la

ಶ ಷ ಸ ಹ ಟ ಈ
sa sa sa ha za ra

Old Karanese

ಅ ಆ ಇ ಈ ಉ ಊ ಋ ಋೂ
a aa i ii uu uu ri rii

ಎ ಏ ಐ ಒ ಓ ಔ ಅಂ ಅಃ
e ee ai o oo au am ah

ಕ ಖ ಗ ಘ ಙ ಚ ಛ ಜ ಝ ಞ
ka kha ga gha na ca cha ja jha na

ಟ ಠ ಡ ಢ ಣ ತ ಥ ದ ಧ ನ
ta tha da dha na ta tha da dha na

ಪ ಫ ಬ ಭ ಮ ಯ ರ ಲ ವ ಳ
pa pha ba bha ma ya ra la va la

ಶ ಷ ಸ ಹ ಟ ಈ
sa sa sa ha za ra

Kannada

అ ఆ ఇ ఈ ఉ ఊ ఋ ౠ ఎ ఏ ఐ
a aa i ii u uu r r e ee ai

ఒ ఓ ఔ అం అః క ఖ గ ఘ ఙ
o oo au am ah ka kha ga gha na

చ ఛ జ ఝ ఞ ట ఠ డ ఢ ణ త థ ద ధ న
ca cha ja jha na ta tha da dha na ta tha da dha na

ప ఫ బ భ మ య ర ల వ ళ శ ష స హ ఱ
pa pha ba bha ma ya ra la va la sa sa sa ha ra

Telugu

Tamil Scripts

Tamil is a Dravidian language spoken by around 52 million people across the world. It is the first language of the Indian state of Tamil Nadu, and is spoken by a significant minority of people (2 million) in north-eastern Sri Lanka, as well as in Malaysia and Singapore. Tamil is an ancient language with Old Tamil spoken from 300 BCE to 700 CE. Middle Tamil spoken from 700 CE to 1600 CE. Modern Tamil spoken from 1600 to the present.

Tamil script evolved from the Brahmi system, although some scholars believe that its origins go back to the Indus script. The earliest known Tamil inscriptions date back to at least 200 BC if not earlier. The oldest literary text in Tamil was composed around 200 BC, using the Tamil-Brahmi script which comes in early Tamil-Brahmi 2nd c. BCE to 1st c. CE, and late Tamil-Brahmi 2nd to 4th c. CE. The Old Grantha script used for writing Sanskrit, seems to be the basis for the modern Tamil script. This is possibly a unique case of sympathetic evolution of two scripts, each adapted to writing a different language, Sanskrit and Tamil.

Vatteluttu

By the 5th century, Tamil-Brahmi had evolved a new script, a local variant called Vatteluttu, Vatteluthu or Vallezhuthu, meaning 'curved letters'. Employed by the Tamils, along side Tamil-Brahmi in old Tamil inscriptions and epigraphs. Tamil-Brahmi for writing Sanskrit and Vatteluttu for writing Tamil. It is the origin of Grantha script, the source of Malayalam, and has sister scripts called Kolezhuttu "straight letters" and Malayamna. Between the 6th and 14th centuries, it replaced Tamil-Brahmi for writing the Tamil language, until the 12th c. CE. when it was supplanted by Tamil-Grantham. It continued to be used into the 18th century in the Chera and Pandya kingdoms.

Grantha

The Tamil language was originally written in the Old Tamil-Brahmi script from as early as 200 BCE. By the 5th century CE, the script had developed into the more rounded Vatteluttu script for writing Tamil. In the 6th century, the Pallava's commissioned the creation of a new script for writing Sanskrit and the classical language of Manipravalam, a Tamil-Sanskrit hybrid. A modified form of Vatteluttu, the Grantha alphabet contains extra letters to write Sanskrit.

In Sanskrit, Grantha literally means "knot" a word used to denote literary works and the scripts used to write them. This stems from the practice of binding inscribed palm leaves using a length of thread held by knots to form books.

There were two main branches of Grantha. Eastern was written in Tamil Nadu in two distinct hands, Jain or round and Brahmic or square. The Western variant or Tigalari, Tulu-Malayalam or Pallava-Chola was popular in the state of Kerala. It also influenced the Indo-Aryan Sinhala script. Some believe that when the Vedas were first written down in the 5th century CE, they were written in Grantha.

Under Pallava patronage the script developed into three distinct varieties, Old Grantha 550-950, Medieval or Transitional Grantha 950-1250 and Modern or Tamil Grantham 1250-1900, the parent script of modern Tamil. These scripts are calligraphically different from the earlier Pallava Grantha script.

Grantha remained in popular use until the 19th century, and is still in restricted use in traditional Vedic schools in the 21st century. The rising popularity of Devanagari replaced Grantha in religious and scholarly texts, while the political pressure for its complete replacement by the modern Tamil script in popular texts, led to its gradual demise in the early 20th century.

Modern Tamil

Originally derived from the eastern variant of the Grantha script during the Pandya dynasty. Over time the script has changed and it was simplified in the 19th and 20th centuries to make Modern Tamil. The alphabet is well suited to writing literary Tamil, or Centamil. However it is ill-suited to writing colloquial Tamil or Koduntamil. During the 19th century, attempts were made to create a written version of the colloquial spoken language. Nowadays the colloquial written language appears mainly in school books and in passages of dialogue in fiction.

Tamil Scripts

3rd c. BCE	3rd c. CE	5th c. CE	7th c. CE	7th c. CE	16th c. CE
Tamil-Brahmi	Pallava	Vatteluttu	Grantha	Tamil-Gramtha	Tamil

development of the initial A grapheme for Tamil

a	aa	i	u	e	ka	na	ca	na

ta	na	ta	na	pa	ma	ya	ra	la	va	ra	la

Vatteluttu

a	aa	i	u	e	ka	kha	ga	gha	na	ca	cha	ja	jha	na

ta	tha	da	dha	na	ta	tha	da	dha	na	pa	pha	ba	bha	ma

ya	ra	la	va	sa	sa	sa	ha	la

Old Grantha

a	aa	i	ii	u	uu	ri	rii	li	lii	e	ai	o	au

ka	kha	ga	gha	na	ca	cha	ja	jha	na	t	th	da	dha	na	ta	tha

da	dha	na	pa	pha	ba	bha	ma	ya	ra	la	va	la	sa	sa	sa	ha

Modern Grantha / Tamil Grantham

a	aa	i	ii	u	uu	e	ee	ai	o	oo	au

ka	ng	ca	ha	ta	na	ta	na	pa	ma	ya	ra	la	va

za	ja	ra	na	sa	ja	sha	ha	ksha	shri

Modern Tamil

Tigalari

Grantha is the name given to specific scripts used to write Sanskrit texts in southern India. Such scripts were developed between the 6th and 14th centuries CE, by the Pallava, Chola and Pandya dynasties. The first form of Grantha was an ornamental version of the Pallava Brahmi script and calligraphically distinct from the later Grantha forms. The second, called Old Grantha, was commissioned and developed from the Vateluttu script by the Pallavas to write Sanskrit texts. This was followed by intermediary and late forms. The late form is also called Modern or Tamil Grantham.

The Sanskrit word, Grantha, literally means "knot" a word used to denote books and the script used to write them. This stems from the practice of binding inscribed palm leaves using a length of thread held by knots. There were two main branches of Grantha. Eastern was written in Tamil Nadu in two distinct hands, Jain or round and Brahmic or square. The Western variant or Tigalari, Tulu-Malayalam or Pallava-Chola was popular in the state of Kerala. It also influenced the Indo-Aryan, Sinhala and Dives scripts.

Tigalari, Tulu

In the 12th century, the western form of Grantha developed into the Tigalari script. It was formally used to write the Malayalam and Tulu languages spoken in Kanarkata and Kerala. Used mainly for religious works, most Tigalari manuscripts are in Sanskrit with some in Kannada and a few in Tulu. Tigalari was replaced by Malayalam and Kannada scripts, although some Tulu speakers still use it to some extent in the Kanara region of Kanakarta.

Evela Akuru and Dives Akuru

Dhivehi or Maldivian is an Indo-Aryan language closely related to, although not mutably intelligible with Sinhala, spoken on the Maldive islands of southern India. Tigalari or Western Grantha derived scripts were once used on the Maldives islands. The early Maldivian scripts were divided into two variants, Evela Akuru or ancient letters and Dives Akuru or island letters, named by HCP Bell in the early 20th century. Evela Akuru being the parent of Dives Akuru which dates back to the 8th century CE. However,

the script is thought to have been used before then.

Dives Akuru was used mainly on tombstones, grants and on some monuments until the 18th century when it was replaced by the Arabic inspired Thaana script. In the southern Madives, Dives Akuru continued to be used until the early 20th century. Today only scholars and hobbyists still use this script also called Dhivehi Akuru.

Malayalam

In the 8th century CE, the Malayalam language was first written in the Vatteluttu script, before it was written in the western Grantha or Tigalari script. By the early 13th century, modern Malayalam had emerged as a systemized script with changes in the mid-nineteenth century

As a result of the difficulties of printing Malayalam, a simplified or reformed version of the script was introduced during the 1970s and 1980s. The main change involved writing consonants and diacritics separately rather than as complex characters. These changes are not applied consistently, so the modern script is often a mixture of traditional and simplified characters. Malayalam is also regularly written with a version of the Arabic, Nashki script, by Muslims in Kerala.

Sinhala

Sinhala or Sinhalese is an Indo-Aryan language spoken in Sri Lanka since the 5th century BCE. Taken there by settlers from India's west coast, with the earliest inscriptions in Brahmi beginning to appear during the 3rd and 2nd centuries BCE. Sinhala emerged as a script in the 7th century and has been in use ever since. The language and alphabet have changed considerably since then. Along the way it has taken influences from the Gupta, Kadamba, Grantha and Malayalam scripts

a aa i ii u uu ru e ai o au am ah

ka kha ga gha na ca cha ja jha na ta tha da cha na

ta tha da dha na pa pha ba bha ma ya ra la va

sa sa sa ha la la

Tigalari / Tulu

a aa i ii u e o ka kha ga ca ja na ta da na

ta da dha na pa ba ma ya ra la va sa sa sa ha la

Akuru Evela

a aa i ee u oo e ey o oa kaa ki kee ku koo

ke key ko koa ka kha ga ca ja na ta da na ta

da dha na pa ba ma ya ra la va sa sa sa ha la za

Akuru Dives

a aa i ii u uu ri e ee ai o oo au

ka kha ga gha na ca cha ja jha na ta tha da dha na ta tha da

dha na pa pha ba bha ma ya ra la va sa sa sa ha la ksa la ra

Malayalam

a aa ae ae i ii u uu ri, ru rii, ruu e ee ai o oo au

ka kha ga gha na nga ca cha ja jha na ta tha da dha na nda ta tha da dha na nda

pa pha ba bha ma mba ya ra la va la sa sa sa/za ha fa

Sinhala

Pali Lipi

Prakrit is the name given to common dialects of Sanskrit. Pali is an Sanskrit dialect, an alternative name for Magdhi Prakrit, the native tongue of Buddha, spoken in Magdha, the land of Buddha's birth, in the foothills of the Himalayas (modern Bihar). As such, Pali is incorrectly used as an umbrella term to catagorize the national scripts of southeast Asia – Burma, Cambodia, Thailand, Laos, and the native scripts of Indonesia, Sumatra and the Philippines – that are derived from the Brahmi abugida.

Pali as a designation is misleading, as it suggests a uniform development and a relationship with the Pali language. However, Pali has no script of its own, in each of the countries where it is used as a religious language, it is written in the national or local script.

The word 'Pali' means scripture and was first used in southern India and Sri Lanka to describe Magdhi Prakrit. As such, Pali is widely studied because it is the liturgical language of the Tipitaka or Buddhist Pali Canon, making it the sacred language of all Orthodox or Theravada Buddhist texts. Theraveda meaning 'little vehicle', as opposed to Mahayana meaning 'great vehicle' and Vjrayana meaning 'diamond vehicle'.

Indian culture spread to southeast Asia from the 1st c. CE with the establishment of Hindu kingdoms in Fu-man and Champa (Cambodia-Vietnam). Pali was initially written in a variety of northern and southern Brahmi variants before it was carried as a written language from southern India and Sri Lanka, to the kingdoms of southeast Asia, during the 7th century with the spread of Theraveda Buddhism.

From the 2nd century, the northern Brahmi variant of Pyu was used to write most of the Mon, Tibeto-Burman and Tai-Kidai languages of Burma. The southern variants of Kadamba, Pallava and Tamil influenced the development of the Khmer, Thai and Lao scripts. The Austronesian Malay language, was written in Pallava and Devanagari before being written in Arabic. Across Indonesia, writing systems evolved from the Pallava script via Tamil, Sanskrit and Mon scripts to write Austronesian languages spoken in Java, Sumatra, Borneo and the Philippines before the arrival of Islam and Christianity.

In southeast Asia, a proportion of the languages are tonal languages, in which each letter can be pronounced in several tones, flat, low, middle, high, to indicate meaning. For which, there are special tonal marks, similar to diacritics, used to indicate the tonal value of a letter. Thai and Lao have no set of initial vowels, instead they use a base sign, a gloteral stop for all vowels with the relevant vowel diacritic attached as a satellite to register its sound value. Diacritic marks form the inner orbit of a letter while tonal marks form the outer orbit.

Pyu / Old Mon (Burma)

Pyu is a Sino-Tibetan language spoken in Burma. The northern Brahmi variant of Pyu, developed from the southern Kadamba-Pallava script between the 2nd and 6th centuries CE. Used in Burma to write Pyu Pali and Pyu Tircul. The source script for the Mon, Burmese, Shan and Lanna scripts.

Ancient Khmer (Cambodia)

Khmer is a Austro-Asiatic language related to Mon spoken in Cambodia, Vietnam, Laos, Thailand and China. Khmer writing shares many similarities with Thai and Lao, that have developed from centuries of two-way borrowing. Khmer script descended from the Pallava script during the 5th and 6th centuries and is calligraphically similar to the Thai and Lao scripts.

Sukhothai (Thailand)

The source script for writing the Siamese language (Tai Siam). Developed from the Pallava script via the Khmer script during the classical Thai period by King Ramkhamaeng in 1283, whose capital was called Sukhothai.

Kawi (Indonesia)

Kawi from "kavi" meaning "poet", the Kawi script originated in Java, developed from southern Brahmi, Pallava script via Tamil, Sanskrit and Mon scripts during the 8th century CE. Used to write the Malayo-Polynesian, Old Javanese language. It spread across southeast Asia to become the parent script of Javanese, Balinese, Batak, Baybayin, Kulitan, Buhid, Hanuno'o, Lontra, Old Sudenese, Rencong, Rejang and Tagbanwa scripts of Java, Bali, Sumatra, Borneo and the Philippines.

Used mainly to write Sanskrit and Old Javanese, the earliest inscriptions in Old Kawi, dated to between 750-925 CE, are found in Java with other inscriptions in Bali and Sumatra. Late Kawi dates between 925-1250. After 1250 its several varieties are usually referred to as Javanese script. The script was in use until the 16th century, replaced by either its descendents, or Arabic or Roman letters.

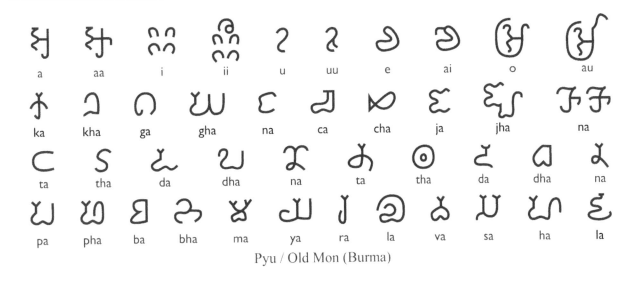

| a | aa | i | ii | u | uu | e | ai | o | au |

| ka | kha | ga | gha | na | ca | cha | ja | jha | na |

| ta | tha | da | dha | na | ta | tha | da | dha | na |

| pa | pha | ba | bha | ma | ya | ra | la | va | sa | ha | la |

Pyu / Old Mon (Burma)

| ka | kha | ko | kho | no | ta | tha | ro | no | jo | jho | tha | no | ja | tha |

| do | dha | na | bo/p | po | pho | mo | yo | ro | lo | vo | sa | sa | so | lo |

Ancient Khmer (Cambodia)

| k | kh | kh | kh | kh | kh | n | c | ch | | k | d | t | th |

| n | d | t | th | ? | ? | n | b | p | ph | f | ph |

| f | ph | m | j | r | l | w | s | s | s | h | ? |

Sukhothai (Thailand)

| k | g | ng | ch | j | ng | t | d | t | d |

| n | p | l | m | y | r | l | v | s | h |

Old Kawi (Indonesia)

Burmese Scripts

Burma is the old name for the country now called Myanmar. Before that it was called Mon, after the people living there. The Mon language, also called Peguan or Talaing, is a member of the Mon-Khmer group of Austro-Asiatic languages spoken in Burma and Thailand. Burmese is a tonal language, a member of the Tibeto-Burman language group.

Burmese letters or Myanmar Akkha are used to write the related languages of Burmese and Karen spoken in Burma and Thailand. Together with the Khmer, Thai and Lao scripts, they are often referred to as a Pali scripts. This is misleading as Pali is a religious language that is written in the national or local script. These scripts evolved from the southern Brahmi variant called Pallava Grantha, in southeast Asia between 700 and 1200 CE in the wake of the spread of Buddhism from southern India and Sri Lanka.

Mon

A non-tonal Austro-Asiatic language spoken in Burma and Thailand. The Mon script developed from the Brahmi derived Pyu/Old Mon script in the 6th century, although Modern Mon maybe derived from Myanmar Akkha, not the other way round.

Peguan

As of the 8th century, the Peguan script served for writing the Mon language. An Indian Brahmi derived script thought to be a mixture of the northern Brahmi variant Pyu amd the southern variant Kannada/Tegulu script.

Burmese

From the 11th century onwards, Peguan evolved into the Burmese script or Myanmar Akkha. The inner form of the Burmese alphabet is that of an Indian-type syllabic alphabet with each consonant letter containing an inherent vowel 'a' with diacritic marks to indicate other vowel values.

Tonality is expressed in Burmese writing using tonal marks to pronounce each syllable in one of four tones – high short falling, low long falling, high long falling and high flat. Some vowel letters have an inherent tone; the low tone remains unmarked; and the other two are indicated by additional diacritics, a double dot for the high long falling tone and an underdot for the flat tone.

From the 12 to the 15th century, the Burmese evolved the Kyok-cha script, with its distinguishing curvilinear appearance, the letters consisting almost entirely of circles. Modern Burmese is a descendent of that script and for this reason it is known as Ca-lonh or 'round script'. Its appearance arising from the practice of writing on palm leaves with a sharp stylus, as straight and angular letter forms were more likely to break the leaf.

Tamarind is the name given to a formal book script, a calligraphic square script style, created by writing on treated palm leaves using a square-nibbed pen and a special adhesive ink made from tamarind seeds.

Shan

Shan is a Tai language, also known as Tai-Yai or Tai Long spoken in Burma, Thailand, Laos and China and related to Thai and Lao. Shan is a round script derived from Mon script with some letters the same as Burmese script, others are are stylistically similar. Few Shan speakers can read or write Shan. Like Thai and Lao, Shan has no initial vowels, using a base sign and vowel diacritics to indicated pronunciation.

Burmese Scripts

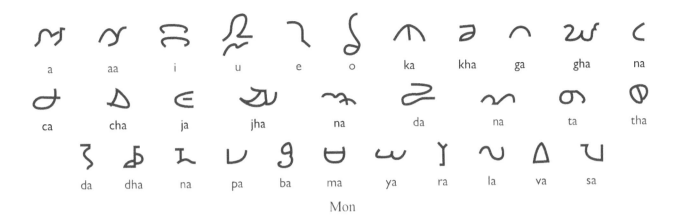

a	aa	i	u	e	o	ka	kha	ga	gha	na
ca	cha	ja	jha	na	da	na	ta	tha		
da	dha	na	pa	ba	ma	ya	ra	la	va	sa

Mon

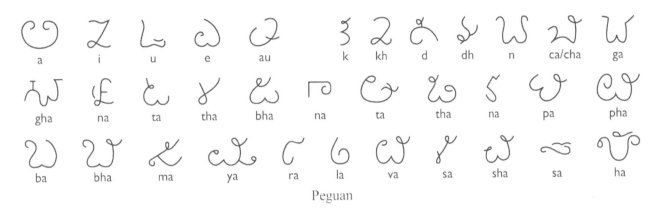

a	i	u	e	au	k	kh	d	dh	n	ca/cha	ga
gha	na	ta	tha	bha	na	ta	tha	na	pa	pha	
ba	bha	ma	ya	ra	la	va	sa	sha	sa	ha	

Peguan

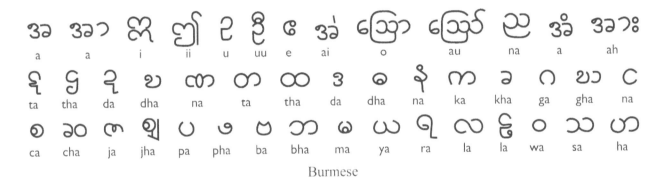

a	a	i	ii	u	uu	e	ai	o	au	na	a	ah
ta	tha	da	dha	na	ta	tha	da	dha	na	ka	kha	ga	gha	na
ca	cha	ja	jha	pa	pha	ba	bha	ma	ya	ra	la	la	wa	sa	ha

Burmese

ဗျြိုင်ဝင်္ဂြက္ဍ၎ပင်္ဂံ ယျြယပ္ပ ၎ောၢ

Tamarind script

ka	kha	nga	tsa	sa	nya	ta	tha	na	pa	pha	fa
ma	ya	ra	la	wa	ha	a	ga	xa	da	ba	

Shan

Khmer Script

Khmer is the national language of Cambodia. The Khmer script developed from the Brahmi Pallava script between the 5th and 6th centuries. The oldest inscription in Khmer dates back to 611 CE. Khmer, together with Burmese, Thai and Lao are often referred to as 'Pali scripts', although this is misleading as Pali is a language without a script.

Khmer is a Mon/Khmer language belonging to the Austro-Asiatic group. It is a syllabic alphabet based on the Brahmi abugida, that shares many features with Thai and Lao as a result of two-way borrowing. The most conspicuous characteristic of the Khmer system is that it makes use of two series of consonant graphemes. Originally these corresponded to the series of voiced and unvoiced phonemes in Indian scripts, but in Khmer they serve a different function. Those in the first series have an inherent 'a' and those in the second series have an inherent 'o'. The inherent vowel is a short 'a' in a syllable without a final consonant, and a short 'o' in a syllable with a final consonant.

Vowels are indicated using either, separate letters or diacritics, which are written above, below, after or around consonants. The pronunciation of the vowels depends on whether the consonant they are attached to is of the first or second series. All consonants have a subscript form which is used to write the second consonant of a cluster. In most cases the subset graphemes are smaller versions of the standard graphemes, but some subscripts no longer bare any similarity with their full-sized counterparts. There are no spaces between words, spaces indicate the end of a clause or sentence.

Old Khmer

Khmer has a literary tradition that goes back to the 7th century CE. Its script is a syllabic alphabet derived from the Brahmi system through the southern Indian Pallava script, which is first attested to in Old Khmer inscriptions dating from 611 CE. Over the centuries a distinct system evolved with some properties not found in other syllabic alphabets of the Indian type.

In Thailand, Old Khmer is called 'Khom (Phasa Khom)'. They consider the script to be extremely sacred and to posses magical power within the letters. It is used for sacred and religious texts, never for common speech or everyday matters. It is traditionally used when inscribing 'kathas', Thai/Pali sacred prayers written on paper, cloth, metal or any other surface including skin for Sak Yant tattoos.

Khmer

Over the centuries, the modern Khmer script has emerged from Old Khmer script. The modern script comes in four styles: Aksar Chrieng meaning 'oblique' or 'slanting' letters, most commonly used for handwriting. Aksar Chhor or Trang meaning 'straight' or 'standing' letters, most commonly used as a typeface. Aksar Khom meaning 'Old Khmer', a palm-leaf script used for Yantras and tattoos. Aksar Mul meaning 'rounded script', referring to its thick, bold, letter style. Used for titles, headlines and royal names.

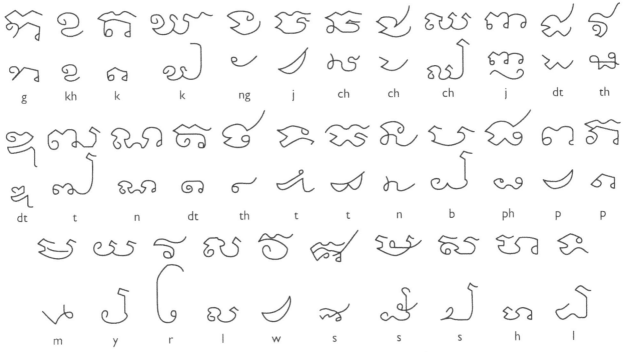

g	kh	k	k	ng	j	ch	ch	ch	j	dt	th

dt	t	n	dt	th	t	t	n	b	ph	p	p

m	y	r	l	w	s	s	s	h	l

Old Khmer / Khom - script and superscript

ka	kha	ko	kho	nyo	ca	cha	co	cho	no	da

tha	do	tho	na	ta	tha	to	tho	no	ba	pha	po

pho	mo	yo	ro	lo	wo	sa	ha	la	vowel

consonants

	1st series	ka	kaa	ke	key	ke	kei	ko	kou	kue	kae
	2nd series	ko	kie	ki	kii	ki	kii	ku	kuu	ku	kai

	1st series	kie	kie	kei	kae	kay	kao	kaw	kom	kah
	2nd series	kie	kie	kee	ke	kiy	koo	kiw	kum	keh

vowel diacritics

Khmer / Chhor (text)

Khmer Mul (heading/display styles)

Thai Scripts

Thai, along with Lao and Khmer are often referred to as 'Pali scripts', this is misleading, as Pali is a language without a script. Thai is a tonal Tai-Kidai language belonging to either the Sino-Tibetan or Austronesian family, as the dispute to its origins continues. Of the 95 Tai-Kidai languages spoken, 62 of them belong to the Tai group.

Tai-Kidai languages originated in southern China and moved southwards around a thousand years ago into Vietnam, Laos, Thailand and Burma. These southwestern Tai languages are split into regional families of northern, central and southern types. The northern group includes Khun, Shan, (Burma) Tai Muang, (northern Thailand) Tai Noi (Old Lao), Tai Dam, Tai Don (Vietnam). Central Tai or Siamese is the official language of Thailand. Southern Tai is also known as Pak Tai or Dambro. Historically, there have been two major script styles used in Thailand, the first, Lanna, is derived from the Old Mon script. The second, Thai Siam, is derived from the Khmer script.

Lanna

Lanna was the name of an independent kingdom of northern Thailand (Chaing Mai) that existed between 1250 and 1558 CE. They spoke the Tai-Kidai, Tai Muang language which shares such strong similarities with Lao, to the point that Siamese Thai's referred to it as Lao. Thai and Lao are mutually intelligible but written in two slightly different scripts, but are linguistically similar. Central or standard Thai Siam is now used to write Thai Muang.

Adapted during the reign of King Mang Rai and named after the kingdom, Lanna is a curvilinear script derived from Peguan/Mon script, to write the northern Thai dialect of Tai Muang, also called Tai Yuan. Used for religious purposes, to write Old Lao, (Tai Noi, Lao Thom), found in old manuscripts and temples in northern Thailand.

From the 13th century, it became a source script for several other Tai dialects including Shan (Tai Yai, Tai Long), and Tai Khun in Burma. In China, the Tai Lue (Kam Tai, Tai Lu, Tai Le, Dai) dialect is written in the New Tai Lue script, developed during the 1950s out of the Old Tai Lue script, which is similar to Lanna and still used in southeast Asia, where it is called Tai Tham or Old Lao. Lanna is the only Tai script to have been inscribed in stone.

Thai Siam

Thai is a Tai Kidai language spoken by the Tai Siam who came to occupy central Thailand and founded its capital of Bangkok. Central Thai is the official language of Thailand. Standard Thai is based on the speech of the educated classes of Bangkok. The Tai Siam are though to have left Gungxi in the Yunnan province of southern China between the 8th and 10th centuries CE. As they moved into southeast Asia, they came into contact with the Indianized civilization of the Theraveda Buddhists of Mon and the Hinduism of Khmer, making Thai culture a mixture of Tai, Indic, Mon and Khmer.

In appearance, Thai script is closer to the Tai Dam script which may have the same Indic origins as the Khmer script. Traditionally King Ramkhamaeng (1275-1317) is credited with having designed a curvilinear script called 'Suthothai' after his capital city. The Suthothai script was succeeded in 1357 by the slightly different 'King Lai Thai script'. It was followed in 1680 by the more angular and pointed letterforms of the 'King Na Rai' script. A more compressed version of this script is the present Thai Siam script.

Thai is a tonal language with five tones, low, falling, high and rising tones, while the flat middle tone is left unmarked. The tone of a syllable is determined by a combination of the class of consonant, (low, middle, high), the type of syllable (open or closed), the tone marker and length of a vowel. It has 44 basic consonants, each with an inherent vowel 'o' in medial position and 'a' in final position. The 'a' is usually found in words of Sanskrit, Pali and Khmer origin while the 'o' is found in native Thai words. The 18 other vowels and 6 dipthongs are indicated using diacritics which appear in front of, above, below of, or after the consonants they modify.

ကၘၐၐၐၐๆ
k   kh   k   kh   ng   c   s   c   s   nga   t   th   t   th   n   t   th   d   th   na

ပ ယ ဝ ဒ ဖ ယ ရ လ ဝ ဟ ဂ ဂ ဂ ဉ ပ ဖ ဍ ဎ ဟ ဃ
p   ph   p   ph   m   j   r   l   w   ss   h   l   xx   kh   b   f   f   j   h   s

Lanna / Tai Muang

Tai Khun   **Tai Lue**   **Tai Tham**   **Tai Dam**

Lanna script and its variants

ก	ข	ค	ฆ	ง	จ	ฉ	ช	ซ	ฌ	ญ	ฎ
g	k	k	k	ng	j	ch	ch	s	ch	y	d

ฏ	ฐ	ฑ	ฒ	ณ	ด	ต	ถ	ท	ธ	น
dt	t	t	t	n	d	dt	t	t	t	n

บ	ป	ผ	ฝ	พ	ฟ	ภ	ม	ย	ร	ฤ	ฤๅ
b	bp	p	f	p	f	p	m	y	r	reu	reu

ล	ฦ	ฦๅ	ว	ศ	ษ	ส	ห	ฬ	อ	ฮ
l	leu	leu	w	s	s	s	h	l		h

consonants

กะ	กา	กิ	กี	กึ	กื	กุ	กู	เกะ	เก
a	a:	i	i:	w	w:	u	u:	e	e:

แกะ	แก	โกะ	โก	เกาะ	กอ
ae	ae:	o	o:	ɔ	ɔ:

เกอะ	เกอ	เกียะ	เกีย	เกือะ	เกือ
oe	oe:	ia	ia:	wa	wa:

กัวะ	กัว	กำ	ใก	ไก	เกา
ua	ua:	am	ai	ai:	au

vowel diacritics

Tai Siam

Cham, Lao and Tai-Viet

The indigenous language of southeast Asia is thought to be Austro-Asiatic. The Cham and Vietnamese speak Austro-Asiatic languages, Malayo-Polynesian and Mon/Khmer respectively. Over time, speakers of Tai Kidai, like the Lao, have made their homes there. The Cham and Lao employ Indian derived writing system, while the Vietnamese have used Chinese characters and the Latin alphabet.

Speakers of Tai-Kidai moved from southern China into southeast Asia around 1000 CE, settling in Burma, Thailand, Laos and Vietnam. Tai Kidai is usual classified as a Sino-Tibetan language, although today it is seen more as Austro-Asiatic. In China, Tai languages are seen as a separate group as of the 95 Tai-Kidai languages, 62 of them are Tai.

Cham

Cham is a Malayo-Polynesian language spoken in Cambodia and Vietnam. The script derived from southern Brahmi around 200 CE, part of the Hindu expansion. The earliest inscriptions in Cham date from the 1st century CE. The Cham script has two variants, western, written in Cambodia, and eastern, written in Vietnam. The Cham language was broken into western and eastern variants by the Vietnamese who were pushing south during the 16th century.

Lao

The Lao language belongs to the Tai subgroup of Tai-Kidai languages. Closely related to Thai, both Lao and Thai languages are written in scripts derived from the Khmer script, which is itself derived from the Brahmi Pallava script. These southeast Asian scripts are classified as Pali scripts, this is misleading as Pali is a language without a script.

Old Lao script (Tai Noi, Lao/Tai Tham) was written in the Lanna script with a simple grapheme inventory of 22 letters of the common Indian type, consonant with inherent 'a' and four independent vowels.

Modern Lao writing was given its present form in a reform carried out in the 1960s. Many irregularities of the old system, such as silent letters in Pali loan words have been abolished, and the spelling system has been adjusted more closely to Laotian phonology.

Lao is a tonal language. The writing system marks tones with four superscript diacritics placed over the consonant graphemes and on top of vowel diacritics, if any. Consonant graphemes are divided into three classes, high, middle and low. In combination with the tone marks they determine the tone of a written syllable. The inherent vowel is phonetically realized as 'a'. Other vowels are indicated by diacritic satellites grouped around the consonant grapheme. These vary in form depending on whether the vowel occurs in medial or final position. Initial vowels are pronounced with a gloteral stop and, accordingly, the consonant grapheme, for the gloteral stop serves as the base grapheme for all syllabic vowels. A special sign is used for repetition.

Thai Viet

Tai-Kidai speakers moved into this Austro-Asiatic speaking region around the 13th century. To write their tonal languages of Tai Dam, Tai Dom and Tai Song, they employed a writing system derived from the ancient Thai, Sukhothai script. It has 31 consonants and 14 vowels and no tonal makers. Today, the writing system is called Thai Viet to encompass all the Tai ethnic groups of Vietnam. In Vietnamese the script is called Chur Thai Co or ancient Thai script..

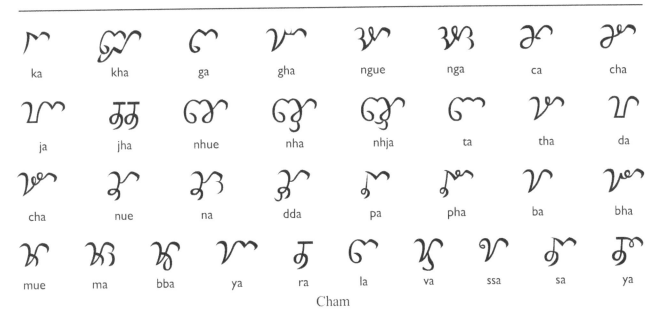

ka	kha	ga	gha	ngue	nga	ca	cha
ja	jha	nhue	nha	nhja	ta	tha	da
cha	nue	na	dda	pa	pha	ba	bha
mue	ma	bba	ya	ra	la	va	ssa	sa	ya

Cham

k	kh	kx	k	kx	kh	ng	c	ch	c	s	ch	ny	t	th	th	n	d	t	th	t	th

n	p/b	p	ph	f	p	f/p	ph	m	y	h	l	w	sh	ss	s	ll	a	h	j	ru	lu

Tai Tham (Old Lao)

a	i	u	e	o

ka	kha	kha	na	ca	sa	sa	na	da	ta	tha	tha	na

ba	pa	pha	fa	pha	fa	ma	ya	ra	la	va	ha	'a	ha

Lao

k	kh	khh	g	ng	ch	ts	s	nh	d	t	th	n	b	p	ph	ph	m	d	r	l	v	h	a

k	kh	khh	g	ng	ch	ts	s	nh	d	t	th	n	b	p	ph	ph	m	d	r	l	v	h	a

Thai Viet (low-top, high-bottom)

Javanese Scripts

Indonesia is a geographical area that includes Malaysia, Java, Bali, Borneo, Sumatra and the Philippines. During the 8th century AD, the south Indian writing system was carried southwards to Sri Lanka before monks and traders took it to Indonesia. The script that accompanied them was the Pallava script, originating in the kingdom of Pallava in southern India. This script was used to write the Austronesian languages of Indonesia. As descendents of the Brahmi writing system all the scripts are abugida's or alpha-syllabic scripts, written left to right. Today, most of these native medieval scripts have been replaced by the modern Indian, Latin and Arabic alphabets

Javanese

Javanese is an member of the Hesperonesian branch of the Malayo-Polynesian family. Javanese is Indonesia's oldest literary language, spoken by its 70 million plus inhabitants. The language has been written in several different scripts, beginning with the Pallava script in the 4th century CE. Between the 10th and 14th centuries, Kawi or Old Javanese had already assumed a distinctive Javanese form. The development from Kawi to Javanese concerns graphic style more than alphabetic make-up.

Following the rise of Islam in Java during the 15th century, Javanese has been written in an adaptation of the Arabic alphabet called Pegon or Gundil script. The Javanese script tradition continued and underwent further changes evolving into its present form in the 17th and 18th centuries. In the 19th century, the Dutch introduced the Roman script for writing Javanese and this has supplanted the native script. Today, few Javanese are literate in the traditional script used exclusively by scholars and for decoration, although it is still taught in schools, and those who can read and write it are held in esteem.

Balinese

Balinese is a Malayo-Polynesian language spoken in Lombok in Indonesia and East Java. The Balinese script is derived from the Javanese script as it crossed from east Java to Bali. The oldest inscriptions dated to the 11th century CE. are copperplate plate reproductions of earlier texts originally written on palm leaves. After the Hindu-Javanese culture of East Java was replaced by Islam, Hinduism re-established itself in Bali during the 16th century. Today, the Balinese language is written in both the traditional script, mainly used for religious works, and in Roman letters.

Sasak

Sasak is a Malayo-Simbawan language of the Austronesian family spoken in Lombok, Indonesia. It is related to the Balinese and Sunbawa languages. Sasak was first written in Aksara Sasak, a derivative of Balinese with Javanese influences. Today it has limited use amongst Sasak speakers who use the Latin alphabet instead.

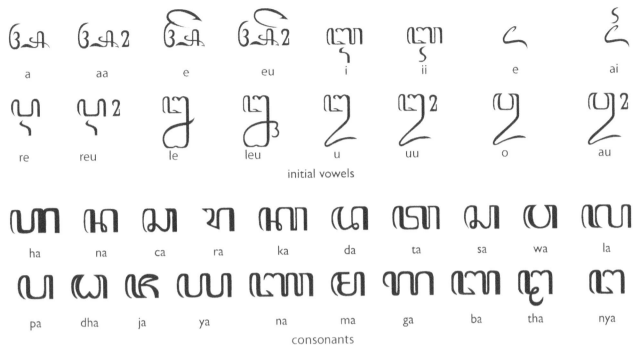

initial vowels

| a | aa | e | eu | i | ii | e | ai |

| re | reu | le | leu | u | uu | o | au |

| ha | na | ca | ra | ka | da | ta | sa | wa | la |

| pa | dha | ja | ya | na | ma | ga | ba | tha | nya |

consonants

Hanacaraka - Jawa aksara

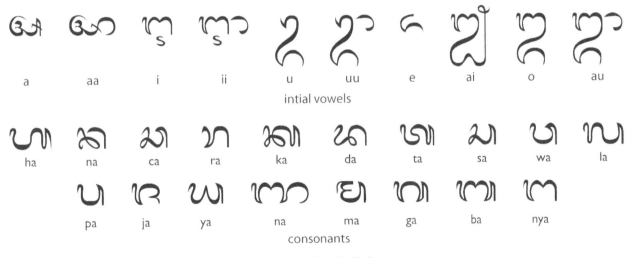

| a | aa | i | ii | u | uu | e | ai | o | au |

intial vowels

| ha | na | ca | ra | ka | da | ta | sa | wa | la |

| pa | ja | ya | na | ma | ga | ba | nya |

consonants

Hanacaraka - Bali aksara

| ha | na | ca | ra | ka | da | ta | sa | wa | la |

| ma | ga | ba | nga | pa | ja | ya | nya |

Sasak

Sumatran Scripts

Sumatra is home to several indigenous scripts of Indonesia, employed to write Austronesian and Malayo-Polynesian languages. A general term applied to any native writing system found in Sumatra is Recong. Many Recong scripts are also known as Sirat Ulu. Recong is often confused with Redjang, which are a specific group of related scripts used to unite various dialects. Recong scripts are ultimately derived from the Brahmi writing system via the Pallava and Kawi script but their outer form is substantivally different. Lontara is one such script in which the letters are written on strips of bamboo placed next to one another and held together by string.

Redjang

A member of the Borean branch of Malay-Polynesian spoken in Sumatra. Redjang is related to Batak and Buginese. It is not to be confused with Rejang-Bonan languages spoken in Borneo, which are quite different. Descended from Brahmi via the Pallava and Kawi scripts, Redjang consists of just 16 letters, consonants with an inherent vowel 'a'. Compared with Kawi, it is much reduced in graphic complexity and the number of graphemes.

Also called Kagagha after its first three letters, the script is native to southeast Sumatra, used to write ritual texts, medical incantations and poetry in Malay and Redjang. Thought to predate the introduction of Islam in the 12th century, the earliest known documents in Redjang are from the mid-18th century. It belongs to a group of scripts called Sirat Ulu or 'upstream scripts' which includes up to seven variants, one of which is Lampung.

Lampung

Lampung is a branch of the Sundik family, a Malayo-Polynesian language spoken in Lampung province of Malaysia and south Sumatra. Today, Lampung is written in Arabic in Malaysia and the Latin alphabet in Sumatra. In the past it was written in its own script known as Had Lampung, which was similar to other scripts used in Sumatra – Redjamg, Bugis and Sundanese. A variety of Surat Ulu script, it was written on bark, palm leaves, metal plates, animal skin, buffalo horn, stone and bamboo. Used to write spells, letters, traditional laws, religious works and poems. Similar to Redjang, Sundanese and Kawi.

Batak

One of several indigenous scripts of the Indonesia archipelago, the Batak script originates from central Sumatra. It is derived from the Kawi script, but its outer appearance is substantionally different. The script was reportedly written from bottom to top in vertical columns arranged from left to right, a peculiarity that has been attributed to the writing surface. It consists of long strips of bamboo placed next to one another and held together by a string. However if the resulting bundle of plates in turned 90 degrees clockwise, an arrangement of right-running horizontal lines results, which may well be a syllabic alphabet of the Brahmi type. Its 18 basic consonants letters have an inherent vowel 'a' which is modified by diacritical marks for other vowels. They are always written separately, without connection.

Lontara (Bugis, Makasserase)

Lontara is a word derived from the Malayan word for the Palmyra palm. Lontar are the leaves which are the traditional materials for manuscripts in India, southeast Asia and Indonesia. It gives its name to a Brahmi derived script used to write several indigenous languages of the Austroneaisn Malayo-Polanesian family that includes Bimanese, Bugis or Buginese, Makasserase, Mander, Ende and Sumbawa, spoken on the Indoneasian islands of Sumatra, Celebes and Lesser Sundas.

Thought to be derived from a common source, a variant of the Kawi script. It came into existence no later than the 17th century, probably earlier, around the 12th century. A syllabic script of the Brahmi type, each of its letters denoting a consonant with an inherent vowel 'a'. Other vowels are indicated by dots placed as diacritics above, below or after the consonantal letters.

The script is written from left to right, however the script is not easy to read as most letters consists of arcs and dots and resemble each other. The similarity of many of the graphemes makes it hard to read. The script was once used to write laws, treaties and maps in Bugis, but now it is only used for marriage ceremonies. Makasserase is still written in Lontara script, although the Latin alphabet is favoured.

Sundanese

A syllabic script of the Brahmi type consisting of consonantal letters with an inherent vowel 'a'. The script of Old Sundanese inscriptions is derived from the Kawi script. The earliest inscription are from western Java dating from the 14th century. Most of the inscriptions were discovered in the Sunda capital and a site east of Jakarta. The date, place and circumstances of the origins of Old Sundanese script are not well understood. It is evidently related to, but differs from, in many ways, the Kawi/Javanese script, which replaced it. Until the 19th century Sudanese was written in the Javanese script. It has also been written in Arabic script called Pegon and in Roman letters by the Dutch.

Sumatran Scripts

Rejang

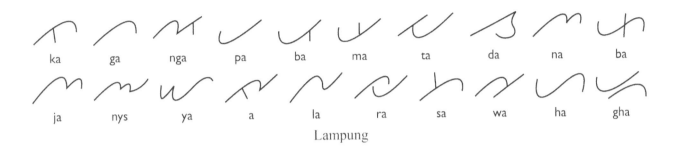

Lampung

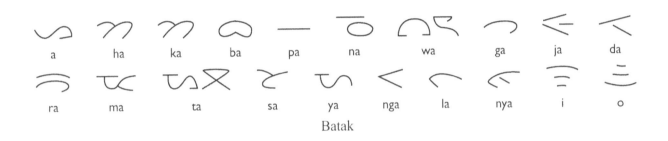

Batak

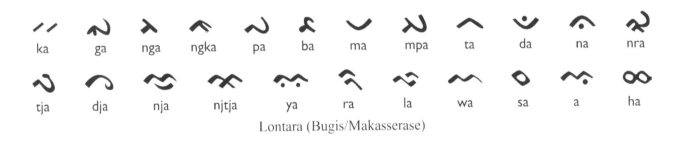

Lontara (Bugis/Makasserase)

Sundanese

Philippino Scripts

The Philippine islands already possessed an established writing system before the arrival of the Spanish in the 16th century. Writing is said to have arrived in Philippines from the island of Boreno during the 9th century or before. It is assumed that migrant Mangyan workers introduced the Kawi script from Indonesia. The earliest documented text in Philippino dates from the 9th century, written in Sanskrit, Old Javanese, Old Malay and Tagalog.

The Philippino writing system is syllabic alphabet descended from the Brahmi script via the Pallava and Kawi scripts. Consisting of consonants with an inherent 'a'. Vowels can be represented by independent or default vowel signs. Diacritics are indicated by dots placed above a consonant for 'i' and 'e', and below it for 'o' and 'u'.

Philippino scripts can be written and read in horizontal lines from left to right, or in vertical columns, either from the top down or the bottom up. Horizontal writing was used to facilitate reading and seen as a result of colonisation. Most of the scripts were in use until the 19th century when they were replaced by the Latin alphabet.

The Spanish documented over a dozen pre-Spanish scripts, leading the Spanish to publish a book called 'Christian Doctrine' using the Tagalog/Baybayin script, thinking it was used all over the islands. In their effort to Christianise the Philippino people, the Spanish destroyed many of their manuscripts which were traditionally written on palm leaves with a stylus or on bamboo tubes with a knife.

Baybayin

Related to Buhid and Mangyan, Baybayin (to spell) is a indigenous script used to write the Austronesian language of Tagalog, the national language of the Philippines. Tagalog comes from the word 'taga-ilog' meaning 'resides beside the river'. It is written in horizontal lines reading left to right, used for personal writings and poetry.

Tagbanwa

Closely related to Baybayin, Tagbanwa is a Malayo-Polynesian language spoken on the island of Luzon. The term is used to denote three languages that are not mutually intelligible. Written horizontantly or vertically, it fell out of use in the 17th century.

Kulitan

An indigenous writing system of the Philippines used to write Kapampangan spoken on the island of Luzon. Written in horizontal lines from left to right and columns reading from bottom to top, but rarely written vertically.

Mangyan (Buhid, Hanuno'o)

Mangyan is a collective name for eight distinct indigenous groups living on the island of Mindoro. Each Mangyan group has its own distinctive language and cultural traditions. However, only the Buhid Mangyans and the Hanuno'o Mangyans have their own syllabic alphabet.

The Mangyan script is found written on 'lukas', bamboo containers for tabaco leaves, bows and arrows, musical instruments, bamboo posts, house walls and woven into palm leaf baskets. Little is known about the origins of this script as the earliest document is from the 19th century. It is proposed that Mangyan and Tagbanwa share common origins with the Tagalog script, an extinct script from the same region because of the many features they have in common. It is written in horizontal lines from left to right and in columns reading from top to bottom.

Philippino Scripts

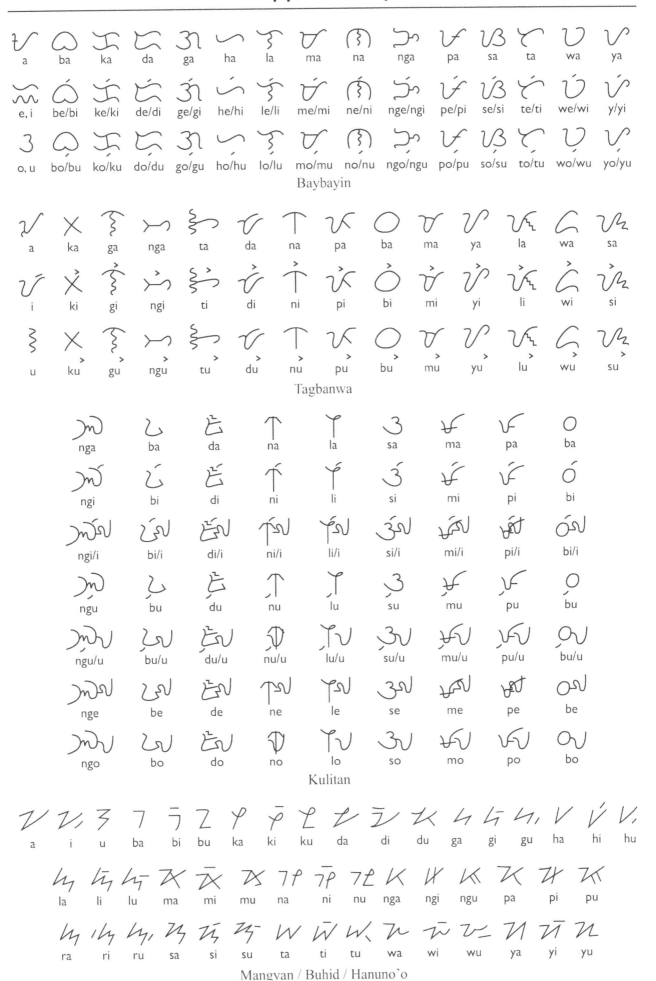

Baybayin

Tagbanwa

Kulitan

Mangyan / Buhid / Hanuno`o

Arabic Scripts

Between the 12th and 18th centuries CE, Islamic invaders settled across the whole of northern India, eventually leading to the creation of the Islamic states of Bangladesh in the east and Pakistan in the west. In these countries the Indo-Aryan languages of Bengali spoken in Bangladesh, and Urdu and Kashmiri spoken in Pakistan are written in a modified Perso-Arabic script called Nasta'liq. Persian having been the official language of the Islamic Mughal government and the most prominent lingua franca of the Indian subcontinent for several centuries prior to British colonial rule during the 19th century.

Nasta'liq and Naskhi

The Nasta'liq calligraphic writing style began as a Persian mixture of scripts called Naskhi and Ta'liq. After the Mughal conquests, Nasta'liq became the preferred writing style for Urdu. It is the dominant style in Pakistan and many Urdu writers elsewhere in the world use it. Nasta'liq is more cursive and flowing than its Naskhi counterpart.

Tamil is also written in a version of the Arabic Naskhi script, known as Awri by Tamil speaking Muslims of southern India and Sri Lanka. It is designed to teach Tamil Muslims to learn Arabic, so that they can read from the Quran and other literary works, to help eliminate poor translation and misreadings. It is not used very often but it is taught in schools.

Khojki

The Khojki script is used exclusively in Sindh in south Pakistan and parts of southeast Asia. Used mainly by Shia Muslims for Ismalii religious literature, as well as literature for a few secret Shia Muslim sects. And is still used to some extent by the Ismalii religious community.

The script was created by Dir Sadaran, a Ismalii missionary who worked with the Hindu, Lohanna community of Sindh during the 15th century. It first appeared in manuscripts in 1737 and was thought to have come from the Landa alphabet during the 16th century. The word Khojki means 'of the master' from the Sindhi word 'khoja' from the Persian word 'Khwajah.' Use to write Arabic, Persian, Sindhi, Punjabi, Gujarati, Urdu and other languages.

Thanna

A vocalized abjad used to write the Indo-Aryan language of Dives or Maldivian, spoken on the Maldive islands. The Thanna script was developed during the 18th century and first appeared in government documents in 1703. It replaced the older Brahmi derived script of Dives Akuru. The origins of the Thanna alphabet are unique among the worlds alphabets.

The first nine letters are derived from Arabic numerals, the next nine letters were local Indic numerals. This means that Thanna is one of the few alphabets not graphically derived from an original alphabet. It doesn't follow the order of other Indic scripts or the Arabic script. The script was originally used primarily to write magical incantations. These included Arab quotations, written right to left. The advantages of using this simplified hidden script were gradually adopted for everyday use.

Thanna almost disappeared in the 1970s. The introduction of new technology, such as the fax machine for which Thanna was unsuitable, made it possible the for the Maldavian Latin alphabet to be quickly implemented in 1976. But the Thanna script was quickly reinstated by President Gayoom in 1978, although Maldavian Latin inscription continues to be widely used.

Arabic Scripts

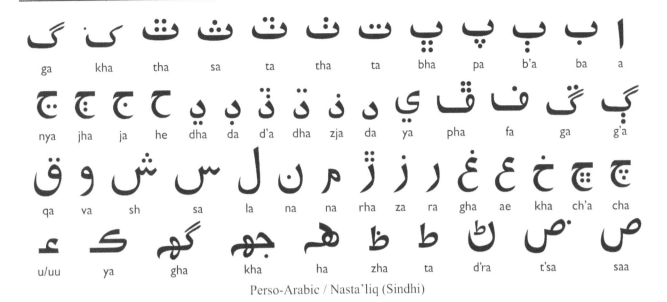

ga	kha	tha	sa	ta	tha	ta	bha	pa	b'a	ba	a
nya	jha	ja	he	dha	da	d'a	dha	zja	da	ya	pha	fa	ga	g'a
qa	va	sh	sa	la	na	na	rha	za	ra	gha	ae	kha	ch'a	cha
u/uu	ya	gha	kha	ha	zha	ta	d'ra	t'sa	saa					

Perso-Arabic / Nasta'liq (Sindhi)

zha	za	p'e	ra	za	da	da	kha	he	cha	ja	s'a	t'a	ta	pa	ba	a
na	ma	la	ga	kha	qa	fa	gha	ae	zha	ta	za	s	sh	sa
ya	yi	ha	wa	va

Arabic / Naskhi (Urdu)

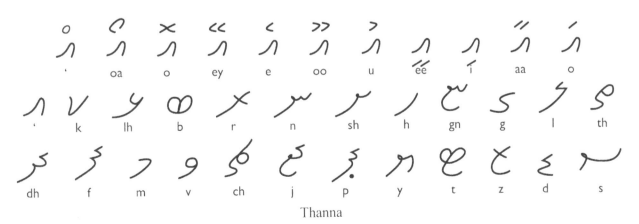

a	aa	i	u/uu	e	o				ka	kha	ga	gha	na
ca	cha	ja	jha	na	ta	tha	da	dha	na	ta	tha	da	dha	na
pa	pha	ba	bha	ma	ya	ra	la	va	sa	ha	la	ksha	jna	ra

Khojki

oa	o	ey	e	oo	u	ee	i	aa
k	lh	b	r	n	sh	h	gn	g	l	th
dh	f	m	v	ch	j	p	y	t	z	d	s

Thanna

Numerals

Indian numerals hold an important position in the history of number development, as they were the first ten digit, place value system, employing numerals for zero and the numbers 1 to 9. This system was adopted by the Arabs which in turn was adopted by Europeans to become the forebears of todays global decimal system.

The advantage of using only ten numerals over other number systems is its economy. The system only requires ten signs ranging from 0 to 9 to write all other numbers. The invention of the zero is very important as without zero, a symbol that represents nothingness-emptiness, we would not have binary code to program computers.

Arabic numerals is the name given to the modern Anglicized number system that is now used by every culture involved in global economics and science. Developed in India and adapted from Arabic in Europe to replace the cumbersome Roman system during the Medieval era.

Brahmi numerals

Before 500 CE, the Brahmi number system was in widespread use across India. In common with all other ancient number systems it lacked the use of a sign for zero and as a result it had individual signs for the tens, hundreds and thousand. But it was the invention of the zero and the place value system that was to revolutionise the Indian number system and turn it into the universal force it is today.

Zero

The addition of zero as a tenth positional digit is documented from the 7th century CE. Although it is most likely that the zero and the place-value system were invented during the Gupta dynasty 240-535 AD. But it is from the Khmer numerals of modern Cambodia where the first material evidence of zero, as a numeral figure, dating it back to the 7th century is found.

Indo-Arabic numerals

Modern Indian numerals are derived from the 7th century number forms which were introduced to Arabia with the arrival of a group of Indian mathematicians in 776 AD. At first, Arab scholars simply copied the signs before modifying them into Arabic style numerals. Over the next two hundred years, Arabic numerals were taken to the Islamic countries of north Africa by Indian, Arab and Jewish scholars and merchants. From north Africa, Islamic culture spread to southern Spain.

After studying Arabic mathematics in Islamic Spain, the prominent scientist Gerbet de Aurillic, the future Pope Sylvester II, brought Arabic numerals back to France in 945 AD. But he did not bring the zero with him and faced severe opposition from European Christians who favoured Roman practises.

By the beginning of the 2nd millennium, the shapes of Arabic numerals brought back by Gerbet were represented by the most fantastic variation on the European mainland. After the Crusades (1095-1270) all those early forms disappeared and the original Arab forms were reintroduced, this time they included the zero for writing algorithms. From this time they established themselves as the standard forms that ultimately give rise to modern Arabic numerals. Making the modern European number system Indo-Arabic in origin

Numerals

Brahmi numerals

Indian numerals - 9-10 th centuries AD

Arabic numerals - 10th century AD

	0	1	2	3	4	5	6	7	8	9
Devanagari
Bengali
Gujarati
Gurmukhi
Oriya / Odia
Telugu
Kannada
Tamil
Malayalam

Sacred Symbols

Indian religion is replete with symbolism, it is said that no other religion employs the art of symbolism as effectively. Most of these symbols are representative of the philosophies, teachings and even the deities themselves. There are two general categories of Indian symbolism. Hand gestures and body position are called 'mudras', icons and drawings are called 'murti'. Of the five major religions of India, two are usually represented by common symbols such as Om, the lotus flower and the conch shell which have similar meanings across its individual sects. The rest use particular symbols related to their faith.

Major religious symbols

A more modern symbol used to represent Hinduism is the Pratik, meaning 'emblem'. It is the symbol of the Ananda Morga 'path of bliss' movement, founded in India in 1959, that places great emphasis on social service along with yoga and meditation. The up triangle symbolizes the external actions of social service. The down triangle symbolizes the internal work of meditation and self-realization. The rising sun is the spiritual progress through the balance of external and internal efforts. The swastika is an archaic sun symbol that dates back to Neolithic times. It is revered by many cultures and found in many forms. The word comes from the Sanskrit word 'Swasti' meaning 'well being' or 'so be it' and symbolizes fulfilment or the ultimate spiritual goal. With its four arms and broken circle the symbol represents the rotation of the sun which makes it a sun wheel. Associations with the number four link it to the material, constructed universe, of order and discipline.

The Tiratana or Three Jewels of Buddhism symbolizes the concept as an eternal flame that holds three circles within it. The three circles represent Buddha, Dharma (teachings) and the Sangha (followers). The Tilaka is a trident symbol of the God Shiva. Its three prongs represent the Trimurti, the three phases of Time, past, present and future, also Heaven, Earth and Hell.

The Parasparopgraho Jivanam is the sacred symbol of the Jain faith, constructed from several other signs and symbols. The outline symbol is called the Lok and represents the Universe, from the top of Heaven through the Earthly plane in the centre to the seven Hells below. The curved arc at the top represents the final resting place of souls or Siddhasila. The three dots or bindhu represent the three jewels of Jainism, Right Faith, Right Knowledge and Right Conduct. The swastika represents the four realms into which the soul may be reborn, as a heavenly being, a human being, an animal being or a hellish being. The hand is a universal symbol for 'stop'. Inside the hand is a circle containing the word 'Ahimsa' which means 'non-violence'. The three symbols together are a reminder to stop and think before acting, otherwise the wheel of birth and rebirth will keep on turning and the soul will never be liberated.

The Khanda symbolise the four aspects of the Sikh faith, as well as encompassing the four sacred weapons within its shape. The double edged sword that gives the Khanda its name is in the centre of the symbol. It stands for the creative power of God and the knowledge of divinity. The circle around the Khanda is called the chakker or wheel, a medieval weapon representing eternity and unity. The daggers at either side of the symbol are called Kirpans. They belonged to the Guru Hargobind and symbolise the balance of spirit and matter.

Astramangala

The Astramangala is a sacred suite of eight auspicious symbols common to a number of Indian religions such as Hinduism, Buddhism and Jainism. In esoteric Buddhism, they are symbolic of Yidam or tantric deities, manifestations of Buddha or enlightened mind, and teaching tools. They were originally used in India at ceremonies such as the coronation of a king.

Different traditions order the eight symbols differently. An early grouping of the symbols included: throne, swastika, handprint, hooked knot, vase of jewels, water libation flask, pair of fishes and lidded bowl. The most familiar set of symbols to Westerners belong to Tibetan or Tantric Buddhism.

The Conch shell is thought to be the origin of the horned trumpet and is attributed to the God Vishnu. The Endless knot is a symbol of the ultimate unity of everything, representing the intertwining of wisdom and compassion. Two Golden fish, often drawn as Carp, represent the auspiciousness of all sentient beings. Originally represented as two rivers, Ganges and Yamuna, associated with the lunar and solar channels which originate in the nostrils and carry the alternative rhythms of breath or prana.

The Lotus flower represents the primordial purity of body, speech and mind, floating above the muddy waters of attachment and desire. The Buddhist lotus bloom has, 4, 8, 16, 32, 64, 100 and 1000 petals. These numbers can refer to the bodies energy centers or chakras.

The Jeweled parasol represents the protection of beings from harmful forces and illness. It represents the canopy of the sky and therefore the expansiveness and unfolding of space and the element of ether. The Treasure vase represents health, longevity, wealth, prosperity, wisdom and the phenomena of space. It symbolizes the Buddha's infinite quality of teaching the Dharma.

The Dharmachakra or 'wheel of the law' represent Gautama Buddha and the Dharma teaching. In some sects this has been replaced by the 'fly whisk' symbolizing tantric manifestations. The Victory banner represents Buddha's victory over the four hindrances, pride, desire, disturbing emotions and the fear of death, in the path of enlightenment.

Sacred Symbols

Pratik
Hinduism

Tiratana
Buddhism

Tilaka
Shivism

Parasparopgraho Jivanam
Jaiinism

Khanda
Sikhisn

major religious symbols

Conch shell

Endless knot

Golden fish

Lotus flower

Jeweled parasol

Treasure bowl

Dharmachakra

Victory banner

Ashtramangla

Om/Aum

The symbol known as Om or Aum is probably the most important sacred symbol of Indic religion. Its variations are found in all of its major belief systems, where it is revered as the ultimate symbol of Creation. Great importance was attached to the word in antiquity. In India, Tantra, the science of the Divine Word in Hindu philosophy, is based on the theory of sound vibration. This philosophy states that the universe is made of sound vibrations, created when the supreme consciousness or Brahman chanted the Bija Mantra of Om, from which all other sound vibrations are manifest.

In the beginning was the Word and the Word was with God. This is how the Bible describes the start of Creation. In Indic religion the Word was OM and God is the Singularity – The One – Brahman. OM is more than a word it is a Bija Mantra, a sound vibration which caused heat, warmth or love to manifest itself as the Flame or Light, in order to illuminate the Darkness, the Void. This metaphysical description of creation has been mankinds prevailing scientific thought throughout the millennia, and it is reaffirmed in the modern scientific Big Bang theory.

The Eternal Syllable/The Primordial Sound

OM is the universal name of the Divine and has different spellings such as AUM and AHM. It was first mentioned in the mystical texts of the Upanishads, associated with Vedanta or Vedic philosophy. OM is not a word but rather an intonation which, like music, transcends the barriers of age, race and culture. It is made up of three Sanskrit letters, A U M, when combined together they make the sound AUM or OM. It is believed to be the basic sound of the world and to contain all other sounds. Tantric Buddhism employs the independent vowel 'A' sign to represent OM.

The supreme consciousness is known as Brahman, from this sphere is born the living cosmos. The cosmos evolves through three stages, creation, preservation and destruction. In the Hindu pantheon, these three aspects are represented by Brahma, Vishnu and Shiva, respectively. Together in their capacity as universal life itself, they are called the Trimurti. This triple aspect of creation is also symbolized in the mantra called OM, in which the three individual sounds A U M correspond to the three stages and gods of the Trimurti, respectively.

Since OM is the expression of the highest faculty of consciousness, these three elements are explained accordingly as three plains of consciousness. 'A' as the waking consciousness or Jagrat.' U' as the dream consciousness or Svapna and 'M' as the consciousness during deep sleep or Susupti. OM as a whole represents the all encompassing cosmic consciousness or Turiya, on the fourth plane, beyond words and concepts, the consciousness of the fourth dimension.

The symbolic meaning of OM remains the same no matter which calligraphic variant OM is written in. Its image is found at the head of letters, the beginning of mantras, in yantras, on pendants and enshrined in every temple and family shrine. The syllable occurs in English in words like omniscience, omnipotent and omnipresent. Thus, OM is used to signify divinity and authority and is akin to the word 'Amen.'

How AUM created the cosmos

Om is the power of sound that brings forth the material world, the concrete universe, composed of the collective sounds of the letters of the Sanskrit alphabet. In the beginning, the mass of the entire creation was contained in one primal star, sometimes referred to as the Singularity – The One. This primal star was undivided awareness and consciousness. Love was the motivation that caused the first movement within the plasma of the star.

The spinning mass of (Sirius B) generated this first sound as it moved into its elliptical orbit at the centre of the primal star. Without movement there is no sound. (love was Gods motivation). The first sound in the creation was/is the first sound of Aum, the A, pronounced as A in America, on the tone F. This first movement and its sound continue to exist as Sirius B and its elliptical orbit. The counter point to Sirius B, counter spin, exists in Sirius A and its elliptical orbit, and generates the second sound of Aum, U, in the tone F". The third sound of Aum, M, is generated by the double helical spiral vortex that extends from the center of the primal star to the top and the bottom. This double helix flow form was generated by and tuned to the movements of Sirius A and B at the centre of the primal star in the tone of G.

When the internal vortex motion and the resulting sound generated by Aum and the F, F", G, tritone reached full resonance, the primal star, suddenly expanded into the infinite detail of the created universe, in the event known as the Big Bang. Aum radiates from the stars of Sirius A and B. Or in simple terms, sound vibration created heat which created light.

| | Bengali | Grantha | Kannada | Malayalam | Tamil |

| Ranjana | Uchen | Javanese | Balanese | Hanzi - Chinese characters |

Om/Aum written in various scripts

the theoretical evolution of aum/om

a u m — au m — au m — aum — om

Hindu
Devanagari

Mahayana Buddhism
Siddhamatrka

Jain
Bangala

Sikhism
Gurmukhi

Aum/Om religious calligraphy

M
Shushupti
destroyer
deep sleep state

Turina
absolute
transendental point

Maya
illusion

A
Jagrat
creator
waking state

U
Swapna
preserver
dream state

the bija AUM
(Akaram Ukaram Makaram)

Stroke order

	Devata	Seed Mantra	Element	Subtle element	Vital air in the subtle body
	Subhadra	Slim	water	taste	Apana
	Balbhadra	Hlim	earth	smell	Prana
	Jagannatha	Klim	fire	sight	Samana
	Sudarsana	Plim	ether	sound	Udana
	Sirhhasana	Dhlim	air	touch	Vyana

Omkara Yantra - a graphic representation of the primordial seed sound Aum/Om, symbolizing the whole cosmos. Aum/Om is split into five shapes to represent the entire universe, resolved into five cosmic principles.

Sabda

Over the millennia, Indic philosophers have devoted a large portion of their time to the study of the creation of the cosmos through sound vibration or Sabda. This is an eastern concept as opposed to the western, whose creation is through light. Both these concepts of Creation are mentioned right at the beginning of the Bible in the lines, "In the beginning was the Word and the Word was with God" and "God said, Let There Be Light" and "Behold there was Light."

All major and lesser known religions promote sound as the origin of the universe. According to Hindu philosophy, Sabda is more ancient than gods and men. It precedes creation, it is eternal, indivisable, creative and imperceptable in its suble form. Sound is what you hear with your ear. Wherever there is motion and vibration of any kind, that is sound. There is movement in all that exists. All movements (and objects) emit sound whether you hear it or not. Atoms in objects spin and make a sound. The planets spin and make sound, these are the individual sounds of the musical scale and when they are heard together they make the sound humans call silence.

Sabda (sound)

The primordial sound Om generates the cosmic energy which spreads like ripples through a pond and becomes the immediate progenitor of the universe. Sabda Brahman is the Father and Nada Brahman is the Mother, the Matrika. She is the originator of five subtle elements, five gross elements, five motor organs, five sensory organs, four karanas, three gunas and the others. Om is Sabda Brahman, all sounds, the audible, unlettered dhvani and the visual, lettered varna are vibrations of Om. The Primordiasl Sound is the most subtle and as it descends from Para Nada (silence), it assumes gross forms eventually resulting in speech (vak, vox).

Dhvani and Varna (audible and visual sound)

Sabda is divided into two distinct forms, audible, unlettered sound called dhvani.and visual, lettered sound called varna. Dhavani or 'mere sounds' includes vocal or non vocal sounds with or without meaning, emitted by men, animals and natural objects, like a roar, thunder, drumbeat, laughter, crying, or expressions of fright, anger etc. Varna or visual, articulated speech can be put down in letters.

A simple explanation of the diference between Dhvani and Varna can be heard when walking along the street listening to traffic, construction, birds, wind, dogs, sirens, alarms, rustling leaves and human conversation, all of which are Dhvani. Only those sounds heard in conversation between people are Varna.

Dhavani is the acoustic aspect of Sabda. It carries vibration, frequency and decibel. This includes the science of pronunciation and chanting (shishka), one of the six Vendangas, and the energy associated with seed sounds, the basis of mantra. Once sound explodes from Sphorta, it is registered by the ear and is deified as Sabda Brahman.

For dhvani to aquire its qualities, the gunas pervade the sound. When the latent mental sound aquires the guna called rajas, she is called dhvani or sound. Dhvani contains the seed sounds, svara or vowels and bija or seed syllables, that make up mantra. The bija or bija-mantra sound 'Om' is dhvani. From Om was derived all the dhavani, the audible, unlettered sounds, and all the varna or visual, lettered sounds.

Varnas are visual, vocal, articulate, meaningful sounds. Once a sound has been made it produces a colour or shade of colour (light). Varna is a Sanskrit word meaning, colour, shade, group, and the sounds of Sanskrit can be ordered by their colour into groups. The term varna covers all visual sounds, including svara and aksara (vowels and syllables).

The combination of varnas to form words, their sequencing and ordering is called vyakarana (grammar). The study of ordinary words is called nirukta. It is based on the physical effect or reaction to various natural phenomena, and the sounds corresponding to those effects. Chandas is the study or meter, the arrangement of syllable groups with diferent lengths. These are three of the six vendangas.

Vak (speech)

Articulated speech or Vak can be visualized by varnas, vocal, articulate, meaningful sounds. The varnas or letter sounds are the body of the Goddess, Matrika, Kali, Kundalini, while Vak is an alternative name for Sarasvati, the Goddess of poetry and eloquence or speech. Each Sanskrit letter has four states of sound.

1. Para-Vak – undifferentiated word. No movement, supreme speech, an indication of sound, it is a sprout.
2. Pasyanti – is creative thought and action by bindhu and abides in the mind. It is the word and the object seen in and by the mind. It is will. The sprout becomes leaves.
3. Madhyana – in the middle between visual and spoken word. It is knowledge. The buds show up.
4. Vaikhari – spoken letter or word. Articulation of letters, words and sentences. Expressed ideas. Chanting of mantras. It is action, It is ablossom.

That Vak (power of speech) which sprouts in Para, gives forth leaves in Pasyanti, buds forth in Madhyana, and blossoms in Vaikhari.

The Classic Sanskrit alphabet starts with an A and ends in Ha (AHA), no matter what language a person speaks, when they suddenly know the meaning of something they will say Aha, the first and last sound of Sanskrit. This is the universal mind saying that it has comprehended something from beginning to end, from A to Z, from A to Ha. When the mind becomes amused, it just repeats the last sound of Sanskrit over and over again, ha ha ha ha ha. Therefore, the Sanskrit word for laughter is Ha or Ha's for multiple laughter.

Sabda

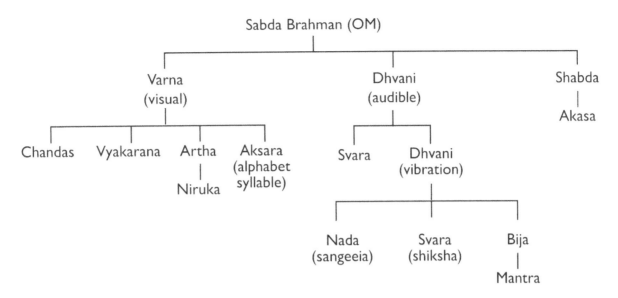

the descent of sound from vibration to audible and visual sound

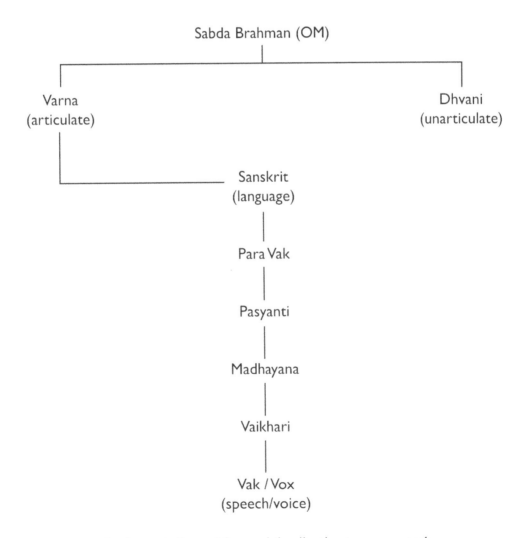

the descent of sound from subtle vibration to gross speech

Varnamala of Bija

Varnamala and Aksaramala are common Indian terms used to denote their alphabet. In simple terms they both translate as 'garland of letters' and represent the alphabet in terms of gross speech. It is the traditional way of arranging the Sanskrit letters according to the phonetic principle laid down by ancient grammarians.

Parallel to the development of the Brahmi writing system was an elaboration of Sanskrit's mystical significance. The fifty one sounds of Vedic Sanskrit were perceived as the Varnamala of Bija, the title of the necklace worn by the Goddess Kali who uses them to destroy, preserve and re-create the Universe.

The fifty one sounds also form the body of the Goddess Kundalini and as such, appear on the lotus petal of the chakras of the human body, they are the sound patterns that create and maintain our organ system. These are the forms in which the mystical or esoteric knowledge of the Vedas is encoded within the Indian alphabet.

Tantric philosophers have devoted a large portion of their vast literature to the explanation of sacred sound, symbol and worship. In Mantra Shastra, the Vedic theory of Universal Creation through Sound is called Sabda. The primordial sound Om (Sabda Brahman) generates the cosmic energy which spreads like ripples through a pond and becomes the immediate progenitor of the universe. This is possible because the primordial vibration returns as primordial variations or Nada Brahman. Creation proceeds from the subtle to the gross as cosmic vibrations (nada). The degree of vibration varies in concentration and wave length, giving birth to what we perceive as light, volume and structure. Sabda Brahman is the Father and Nada Brahman is the Mother, the Matrika.

Hindus believe that Vedic Sanskrit is a language of dynamism, that the fifty one sacred sounds are three dimensional fractal sound formulas that can resonate into being all the possible constructs and processes in Creation. All physical forms are vibratory sound resonance fields, and are contained within the fifty one astral sound forms of the Goddess language. The Goddess creates the Cosmos with these fifty one sounds and their combinations. Aum, the Sri Yantra, the Goddess and her language are one thing.

As Sarasvatti is the Goddess of speech and Vak is the Goddess of the voice, Kali is the keeper of the mother tongue, the Sanskrit language and its letters, its words, mantras and shashtras. Kali's large, red, protruding tongue representing the mother tongue.

The fifty one sacred sounds are shown as fifty one different postures of the Goddess, symbolizing the written forms of the Vedic sounds. Each sound represents a form of divine feminine energy, a form of Shakti (matrika shakti). Called matrikas 'little mothers' they are the individual goddesses that together make up the body of the Mother Goddess. The matrikas represent the universe of names and forms, that is speech (sabda) and its meaning or object (artha). This is why the Goddess Kali wears the Varnamal of Bija.

The Varnamala of Bija is a necklace of skulls or severed heads, each having one of the fifty one letters inscribed upon it, together they represent infinite knowledge. As a garland it represents the inter-connectedness of all Creation. Different names are used to describe it. As the Mundamala, Kapalamala or Rundamala, it is the Garland of Skulls or Severed Heads, numbered at 108, an auspicious number in Hinduism. Representing dominion over, and the power of words and thoughts, of all knowledge. A characteristic of the fierce aspect of the Mother Goddess and the God Shiva. In Tibetan Buddhism it is worn by wrathful deities. It has the same number of beads as a Japamala or rosary used for counting repetition in mantras.

As the Varnamala of Bija, it is symbolic of the origin of sound, signifying Kali is Sabda Brahman, the source of Creation, representing victory over Time and Death, the continual creation and destruction cycles of human existence. The Sanskrit word 'kal' means 'to count' or 'to measure'. The name Kali is the feminine of Kala or Time. Hence Kali can be understood as 'action through time'. Time is the womb from which all Creation occurs. From this womb, Kali as the Mother Goddess brings forth all of Creation.

Therefore, Kali devours all Time or Kala and then resumes her own dark formlessness, that is, the names and forms which the letters signify, the dualism in consciousness, which is creation, vanishes. There is neither "I" (Aham) nor "This" (Idam) but the one non-dual Perfect Experience which Kali in Her own true nature (Svarupa) is. In this way Her Garland is understood, wearing the sounds which she as the Creatrix bore and she as the Dissolving power takes to herself again

red

blue

black

green

purple

white

Varna - colour, shade, class, group

In the Matrika Chakra, the Varnamala of Bija consists of 14 vowels or svara, all coloured red. They contribute Matra or meter and timing to the words and the mantras. Within the 36 aksara, Vyanjana or consonants, the vowel/consonants *am* and *ah* are blue. The 25 mute-consonants called sparsa, are the five vagas beginning with ka, ca, ta, tta, pa, are all coloured black. The ya-varga is coloured green and the sa-varga is coloured purple. The single ligature or samaksara, ksha is white, bringing the total number of letter in the alphabet to 51. Om is red making 52.

Varnamala of Bija

Along with ancient Egyptian, Hebrew, Tibetan and Chinese, Sanskrit is one of the five Holy languages of man. The root language of all Indo-European tongues. Hindu's and Buddhists's believe that all words in Sanskrit are derived from root syllables called Bija. They conceive the Sanskrit alphabet as a matrix, used as a collation tool for the assembly of written information into a standardized order. Their system is ideal for forming new words, eliminating the need to borrow words or scientific terms from other languages.

Sanskrit is considered to be a Goddess language and there are several common Indian terms that are confused when used to describe its letters. The term bija relates to the seed sounds that are the basis of mantra. The term matrika refers to the cosmic feminine energy or Shakti, that is the subtle form of gross speech or varna. The terms varna and aksara are used in relation to the classification of the gross form of the sounds of the Sanskrit language or speech.

The diference between varna and alsara is, varnas cannot be split, 'a' and 'k' or vowels and consonants are varnas. Aksara are syllables, combinations like 'k' and 'a' to make 'ka'. Once a syllable is shaped it is indivisible. The situation is further confused by the use of compound terms such as Bijaksara and Matrikaksara, used to denote the written form. Varna and aksara are classified into two types – svaraksara or vowels, usually shortened to svara, and vyanjanaksara or consonants, shortened to vyanjana. Svaraksara are also known as Pranaksara, ie. they are the main sounds in speech. The ayogavahah, am and ah, are considered to be svara as well as aksara, they are vowel-consonants.

Vana

The purest vibrations are the varna, the imperishable letters (aksara), which are revealed to us, imperfectly, as audible sound (dhvani) and visible form (rupa). These sounds and forms are provisional, a reflection of the immutability of the varna. Varna are to ordinary sounds and letters as atoms are to matter. The varnas are identified with God's Primal Energy (Om), 'the Gods are the seed of the world', the letters developed from the seeds. It is the varnas that bring about Life.

According to the Mantra Shashtra, varna or articulated speech (meaningful sound) is visual in that it can be seen in colour. Generally, the term varna can mean "the separation of the suns rays or energies", used to describe the shape, sound and colour of the letters of the Sanskrit alphabet. Their vana (colour – class, category) is determined by the guna or quality associated with the sound. Guna is not be confused with gana.

Commonly, the units of vak or speech are referred to as vanas. This means they are the basic sounds, the phonemes, they are the units of speech. On a deeper level, the varnas are the units of shape or form, units of colour and they are the units of sound that appear as aksara, letters/phonemes to our ears.

There are seven basic varnas, a, e, u, ae, o, aM, aH. These seven flavours are the primordial variations of the Nada that originate in Muladhara as Vak or speech. Of these 'a' is the beginning, and is called 'varnadi' or 'first of vanas'. 'H' originates from above the others and gets mixed with 'a' produced at Muladhara to produce 'aH'. In Hinduism, these sounds are called the Saptamatrkas. These are the basic forms of sounds. These do not need any intervention of the tongue to be produced. The other vowels ai, ou, au, are combinations of these.

Svara

Svar is the name of the Sun, the shining light, svara are the shining sounds. Vowels or svara are both varna and aksara. Svara are the speech sounds which can form a syllable and can be pronounced independently. Within the svara, there are two groups of 'bouquet of mantra', the hrusva svara – a i u ru lu E O are lunar and the deergha svara – A I L U ai ou aM aH are solar. They are the seeds of creation from who manifest the moon and the sun, Am and Ah respectively, giving rise to light, air, and space, also the five great elements, strength, potency, enlightenment, power (shakti) and resources. These are the rays emanating from the Goddess. The point or Bindhu is the basis of all Creation and the Goddess as mantra – rupinis – appear as the Aksara Brahmi. Almost a million mantras are formed from these syllables, each with a specific power, creating, sustaining, dissolving and merging.

Aksara

Svara are solar symbols, aksara are lunar symbols – the reflected light of the sun. Aksara or akshara means ''imperishable, entity', 'atoms of speech'. The imperishable aksara seeds each letter of the alphabet and becomes manifold. These voiced syllables, structured into words and sentences, give rise to action or Aksara Brahma.

The term aksara is commonly used to denote the whole alphabet, some may confine that to just 34 consonant syllables, others confine their number to 25, the amount of mute-consonants or sparsa, the reflected sounds that form a 'magic square' of Sanskrit phonemes. The remaining consonants, the semivowel or anthastha represent the bija mantra of the lower four of the seven chakras. The sibilants, sha, ssha and sa are Shakti, the energies that manifest the universe, their consorts are Brahma, Vishnu and Shiva. Ha is the bija mantra of the throat chakra.

Varnamala of Bija

Letter	Sound	Gender	Guna/Quality	Deity	Colour	Boon
अ	a	M	rajas	all deities	red	
आ	aa	F	sattva	Parasakti	white	
इ	i	M	tamas	Vishnu	black	
ई	ii	F	rajas	Maya Sakti	yellow	
उ	u	M	tamas	Vaatsu	black	
ऊ	uu	F	tamas	Bhumi Devi	black	
ऋ	ri	N	rajas	Brahman	yellow	
ॠ	ree	N	rajas	Sikhandi	yellow	
ल	lri	N	sattva	the Asvins	white	
ए	e	M	rajas	Virahadra	yellow	bestowing siddhas
ऐ	ai	F	sattva	vital essenceof speech	-	
ओ	o	M	sattva	One supreme god	sunlight	bestowing truths
औ	au	F	sattva	Adi Shakti	white	perfection in every area
आं	am	M	rajas	the Great Lord	red	
आः	ah	F	rajas	Kalarudra (time)	red	

Shiksha correspondences for the a-varga or svara (vowels)

Varnamala of Bija

In ancient India, the Sanskrit alphabet was intimately connected with stories of creation and with early models of cosmology. One starting point of the system were the five fundamental elements (ether, air, fire, water, earth). This evolved into a complex system. The 14 vowels were spirit and the 36 consonants were matter. These 36 consonants (thirty four vyanjana and two ayogavahah) became linked with 36 elements (tattvas) and associated with the 12 solar signs. Key combinations of vowels and consonants became seed letters (bija) and linked with the 7 chakras in the body, the seven planets, the 7 days of the week etc. This idea formed a starting point for oriental cosmology.

European cosmology seemed entirely independent of this Indian model. Recent studies have demonstrated that the 22 letters of the Phoenician alphabet are linked with Chinese astronomy and thus confirm that there was important interplay between East and West. A study of Indo/Chinese magic squares reveals a key to the underlying structure of Western alphabets.

In the West, the vowels of alphabets and elements also played a central role in cosmology. Instead of 14 vowels, the Western system typically used 7 or 5 vowels. The system of 5 vowels became linked with the 5 elements and a foundation for cosmologies ranging from those of ancient Greece to those of the Celtic world. As in India, these links between vowels and elements become a basis for Western religion. In Europe, something else also happened. Systematic study of combinations of the elements became a basis of disciplines of knowledge and eventually led to modern science.

Tattvas

According to ancient Indic philosophy, the universe is made up of 36 elements known as tattvas. Tattva means reality, truth, an element or aspect of reality, conceived as an aspect of a deity. The number of tattvas varies, together they are thought to form the basis of all our experience. Samkhya has 25. Shivaism has 36. Tamil Siddha has 96. Hindu Tantra has 5 and in Buddhism they are the list of Dharmas which constitute reality.

In Shivaism, the 36 consonants (thirty four vyanjana and two ayogavahah) of Vedic Sanskrit represent the 36 tattvas. The 14 vowels are Shakti, the whole being the Universe as sound. The 36th tattva being Shiva/Shakti. The universe begins with the Shiva tattva, within it are five energies which are encoded within the vowels of Sanskrit.

The first energy of the highest (anuttara) consciousness is represented by the vowel 'a'. The second energy is the blissful state of ananda represented by 'aa'. The third state is the subtle state or iccha represented by 'i', The gross state of will is represented by 'ii'. The fourth is the energy of knowledge or janna, represented by 'u'. The 'uu' refers to the appearance of a lessening. The fifth energy of the Shiva tattva is kriya, the energy of action represented by the last four vowels, e,ai,o,u, representing degrees of vividness.

The tattvas are the five gross elements, earth, water, fire, air, ether which are assigned the Ka-varga. The Ca-varga contains the five senses or Tammatas of sound, taste, form, touch and smell. The Tta-varga are the five motor organs, generation, evacuation, ambulation, grasp, speech. The Ta-varga are the five organs of sense,ears, tongue, eyes, skin, nose. The Pa-varga are limited experience, mind, ego, buddhi, Prakriti, Purasha.

Varna Shiksha

The magical symmetries of the Sanskrit alphabet are found in various Hindu and Buddhists texts. The Hindu correspondences come from a very old Sanskrit text found by accident, unlabeled and mis-catalogued in a university in Mysore. Named Varna Shiksha, it describes a number of qualities of letters of the Sanskrit alphabet previously lost. Making the Varna Shiksha a precious jewel in the treasury of knowledge.

In the mislabelled Varna Shiksha, the letters of the Sanskrit alphabet are categorized into gender, male, female and neuter and divided into 'qualities' called 'gunas' used by Hindu's to catagorize behavior and natural phenomena. There are three gunas – sattavas, rajas and tamas. Sattavas have the positive qualities of balance, harmony, goodness, purity, etc. and are white in colour. Rajas are red in colour and have the active qualities of passion, moving, dynamic, ego, etc. Tamas are blue/black and have the negative qualities of imbalance, disorder, chaos, viciousness, ignorance etc.

The vowels, a, i, u, e, o, am, are male. aa. ii, uu, ai, au, ah, are female. Aa, ai, o, au, are sattavic. A, ii, ri, rii, lri, e, am, ah are rajas. I, u, uu, are tamas. The consonants are categorized into gender depending on their position in their varga. The first and the third letters, ka, ga, ca, ja, ta, da, ta, da, pa , ba, of the vargas, plus sha and ksha are male. The second and fourth letter kha, gha, cha, jha, tha, dha, tha, dha, pha, bha, of the vargas, plus ssha and sa are female. The last letter of each varga, na, na, na, na, and ma, the four letters of the ya-varga, ya, ra, la, va plus ri, lri, ha and la are neuter.

Gunas

The Sanskrit word 'guna' means string, thread, strand or virtue, merit, excellence or quality, peculiarity, attribute or property. The three gunas, sattvas, rajas and tamas, are used to understand or interpret natural objects, beings or occurrences. For example, a large stone or a person with destructive tendencies is viewed as tamasic. A thunderstorm or a naturally agitated person is thought to be rajasic. A fresh orange or a naturally peaceful individual is considered sattvaic. If the individual feels the pull of one guna more than another, it is believed that, as humans, one has the ability to change its level through meditation, lifestyle choices and spiritual practises.

Varnamala of Bija

Letter	Sound	Gender	Guna/Quality	Deity	Colour	Boon
क	ka	M	rajas	Prayapati	yellow	granting rain
ख	kha	F	sattva	River Ganges	white	destroying evil
ग	ga	M	rajas	Ganesha	red	destroying obsticles
घ	gha	F	sattva	Bhairava (Shiva)	white	destroying enemies
ङ	na	N	-	Time	black	Torksyam
च	ca	M	tamas	Candra Rudra	black	extolling all around
छ	cha	F	tamas	Bhadrakali Ma Diva	red	bringing victory
ज	ja	M	rajas	Jambhaha	red	
झ	jna	F	tamas	Ardhanansam	black	
ञ	na	N	rajas	snake deveta	yellow	
ट	tta	M	rajas	Bhrngisam	red	
ठ	ttha	F	sattva	Moon	white	
ड	dda	M	raja	One eyed	yellow	death destroying
ढ	ddha	F	raja	Yama	blue	fulfilment of intention
ण	nna	N	raja	Nandi	red	
त	ta	M	sattva	Vastu Devata	white	
थ	tha	F	sattva	Brahman	black	granting of mastery
द	da	M	raja	Durga	black	accomplishment
ध	dha	F	raja	wealth-bestowing	yellow	destroying evil
न	na	N	sattvas	Savitri	crystaline	

Shiksha correspondences for the ca, tta and ta vargas

Varnamala of Bija

The concept of gunas originated in Samkhya, one of the six Astika schools of Hindu philosophy. It is most related to the Yoga school of Hinduism. This dualistic philosophy records the universe as consisting of two realities, Purusa – consciousness, and Prakriti – mother. Jiva, a living being is that state in Purusa bonded to Prakriti in some form.

This fusion led to the emergence of Buddhi – intellect, and Ahankara – ego consciousness. Samkhya also describes the universe as one created by Purusa/Prakriti entities, infused with the various permutations and combinations of various enumerated elements, senses, feelings, activity and mind. During the state of imbalance, one or more of the constituents overwhelm the others, creating a form of bondage particular to the mind. The end of the imbalance is called liberation or Kalvalya.

Prakriti is the first cause of the manifest material universe – of everything except Purusa. Prakriti accounts for whatever is physical with mind and matter cum energy force. It is the first tattva or principle of the universe. It is composed of three escated characters or tri-gunas called Sattva meaning goodness, constructive, harmonious. Rajas means passion, active, confuse. Tamas means darkness, destruction and chaotic. All of these gunas are present in everyone and everything, it is the proportion that is different.

The Upanishads is one of the earliest texts making reference to the relationship between the Trimurti and the three gunas as creative/activity, preservation/purity, destroyer/recycler. The idea that three types of guna, innate nature and forces that together transform and help changing the world is, however found in numerous earlier and later texts.

As Shiva's wife, Kali is the embodiment of the three gunas or 'principles of nature – sattvas, rajas and tamas'. She creates with sattvas – goodness and purity, preserves with rajas – passion and action, and destroys with tamas – ignorance and inertia. Her white teeth symbolize sattva or serenity. Her red tongue symbolize rajas or activity and her drunkenness as tamas or inertia, meaning tamas can be conquered by rajas and rajas by sattvas.

Varnamala of Bija

Letter	Sound	Gender	Guna/Quality	Deity	Colour	Boon
प	pa	M	sattva	Porjonya (rain)	white	granting perfection in rain
फ	pha	F	-	land of cattle	black	destroying evil
ब	ba	M	raja	Trimurti	red	mastery of all things
भ	bha	F	raja	Bhorgava	red	good fortune
म	ma	N	tamas	God of Love	black	the fruit of one's desire
य	ya	N	tamas	Vayu (air)	black	raining upwards
र	ra	N	rajas	deveta of vehicles	red	
ल	la	N	rajas	Prithiri (earth)	yellow	attainment
व	va	N	sattva	Varuna	white	destroying unity
श	shha	F	rajas	Lakashimi	gold	
ष	sha	M	rajas	dvadasatma	red	granting victory
स	sa	F	rajas	Shakti	red	creating stability
ह	ha	M	sattva	Shiva	white	
ळ	la	N	raja	Atma (self)	red	bestowing all powers

Shiksha correspondences for the pa, ya and sa vargas

1) Vasini अ आ इ ई उ ऊ ऋ ॠ ऌ ए ऐ ओ औ आं आः

2) Kamesvara क ख ग घ ङ

3) Modini च छ ज झ ञ

4) Vimala ट ठ ड ढ ण

5) Aruna त थ द ध न

6) Jayini प फ ब भ म

7) Sarasvatti य र ल व

8) Kali (Kaulini) श ष स ह ळ

Goddesses of the eight vargas

Matrika

The Sanskrit word 'Matrikas' means 'little Mothers'. In Hinduism, they are portrayed as a collection of female deities who always appear together in groups of various sizes, 1, 7, 8, 14, 16, 34, 50, 51 and 52. They originated in pre-Aryan, Indus folklore as local goddesses, who protect village boundaries and fertility, taking care of child growth, diseases etc., as extensions of the Mother Goddess. In Devi lore or goddess worship, they all converge together to project one Great Mother Goddess – Mahadevi.

At some point in time during the Muaryan empire, they were seen as 'effecting children', hindering the process of birth and child growth. In the Kushan era, the Matrikas became entwined with the myth of Skanda. During the Gupta era, this link was reinforced further when Skanda was adopted by Gupta warriors, and the Goddesses associated with him gained prominence.

In the Purana manuscripts of the Gupta era, the Matrikas were warrior goddesses who emerged from the various parts of the Devi, to help her in the fight against demons. Seen as a dangerous group of female spirits or goddesses with a malevolent nature. Somewhat similar to that of the Goddess Kali, also described as a Matrika, who fought Raktabija and his demons wearing the Varnamala of Bija.

In the philosophy of Mantra Shastra, Sabda Brahman (Om), emanates the primordial vibration which returns to him as primordial variations in the form of his wife Nada Brahman, her body being the cosmos formed by the 51 vibrations that are the sounds of Vedic Sanskrit. Each sound being an individual aspect of the Mother Goddess or Matrika (Mother). She is said to be the source of everything made of words, mantras and shashtras.

In Tantra, the 51 sounds of Vedic Sanskrit, from A to Ksha of the Varnamala of Bija, have been described as the Matrikas themselves. Together they constitute the body of the Goddess in the form of sound. The Matrika represent the universe of names and forms, that is speech (sabda) and its meaning or object (artha).

The Matrikas are the subtle (mystical) forms of varna or articulated speech. The term Matrika can also means a storehouse of sound syllables, and logos, as the Mother of the spoken word (vak-devi). All we think, imagine, desire, aspire, and dream, begin here.

In Tantra, the embodiment of feminine forces or Shakti are called Matrika, referring to groups of Mother-like deities, the personified energies of the Goddess or Deva-Shakti. Each goddess is represented by a diagram, a posture of herself. The 51 Vedic sounds are shown as 51 different postures of the Goddess, symbolizing Matrika, the Goddess forms of Vedic Sanskrit, believed to posses magical power. Together, the sound and the diagram are Matrika.

It is believed that the letters of the Sanskrit language emanated from the Mother and she takes her name in everyone of them. For the purposes of daily recitations, each of the 51 letters/matrika is extended, in the given order, into the name of a Devi:- Amrita, Aakarshini, Indrami, Iishani, Uma, Urdhva-keshini, Ekapadini, Aishvari, Omkarini, Aishadhantika, Ambika, Aksharatmika, Kalarati, khatita, Gayatri, Ghantadharini, Nanatmika, Chanda, Chaya, Jaya, Jhankarini, Jnanarupa, Thankahasta, Thamkorum, Damri, Dhamkarini, Namini, Tanasi, Thamini, Dakshayani, Dhatri, Nanda, Parvati, Phatkarini, Bandhini, Bhadrakali, Mahakaya, Yashasvini, Rakta, Lambobosti, Varada, Shashini, Sarasvatti, Hamsavathi, Kshamavathi. Matrikas are the binding energies that makes it possible to understand words or symbols strung together as language.

Sapta and Ashta Matrika

Depending upon the philosophy, Matrikas can denote a single character or the entire collection of characters or alphabet. In southern India they are worshipped as the 'saptamatrka' or 'seven mothers.' In Nepal and Tibet they are venerated as the 'ashtamatrkas' or 'eight mothers.'

The number of Matrikas is determined in the structure of the Brahmi abugida, which is arranged into seven and eight individual groups of letters called vargas. First is the 'A' group containing vowels. The Matrikas can be identified with 14 vowels plus the anasvara and visarga making their number 16. The saptamatrka or seven mothers correspond to the seven consonantal groups headed by Ka, Cha, Ta, ta, Pa, Ya and Ksha. If the vowel group is added, they become the ashtamatrka or eight mothers.

Matrika Nyasa

During the ritual worship of the Mother, her presence is invoked in the body of the Sadhata through a procedure known as anga-nyasa or consecration of different parts of the body. The invoking of the Mother – matrika nyasa -along with the five elements is a significant ritual. It is meant to emphasise that you belong to the Mother and that you are sanctified by her presence in you.

In Matrika Nyasa, the letters of the Sanskrit alphabet are placed on the body – head, face, hands, anus and legs. As this is done, the practitioner uses various hand gestures (mudras). The letters are prefixed with Om and suffixed with namah. A more specialised installation of Matrka Nyasa combines the installation of the most powerful set of all letters with the bija HRIM of the Goddess known as Ada Shakti or Durga, the supreme body of the universe, the consort of Shiva. This ritual differs from Kundalini Yoga, in which certain letters are grouped together with each one of the chakras, the seven psycho-physical centers on the human body.

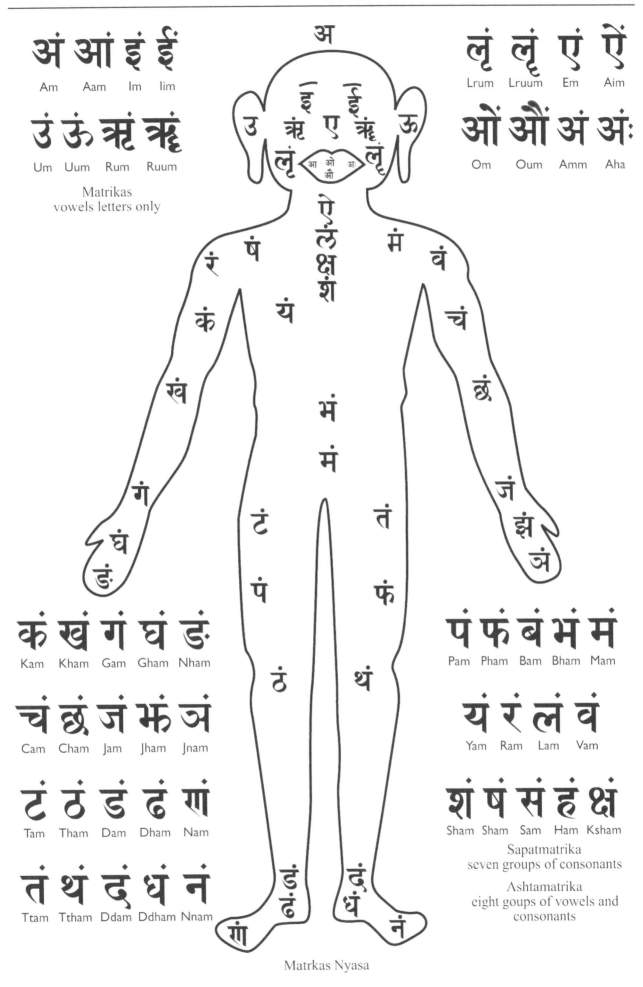

अं आं इं ईं
Am Aam Im Iim

उं ऊं ऋं ॠं
Um Uum Rum Ruum

Matrikas
vowels letters only

लृं लॄं एं ऐं
Lrum Lruum Em Aim

ओं औं अं अंः
Om Oum Amm Aha

कं खं गं घं ङं
Kam Kham Gam Gham Nham

चं छं जं झं ञं
Cam Cham Jam Jham Jnam

टं ठं डं ढं णं
Tam Tham Dam Dham Nam

तं थं दं धं नं
Ttam Ttham Ddam Ddham Nnam

पं फं बं भं मं
Pam Pham Bam Bham Mam

यं रं लं वं
Yam Ram Lam Vam

शं षं सं हं क्षं
Sham Sham Sam Ham Ksham

Sapatmatrika
seven groups of consonants

Ashtamatrika
eight goups of vowels and
consonants

Matrkas Nyasa

Bija

In Indian philosophy, the Vedic language has its roots in a divine primordial language. This root language consists of single syllable sounds called bija, pronounced beej, meaning seed or germ. Bija have multiple meanings and indications depending upon their intonation and the intention with which they are used. These seeds cannot be translated into a literal meaning but have the power to create great transformative growth and expansion in humans at the physical, emotional and spiritual levels.

Out of the bija or root language arises the language of the Vedic texts, which is already differentiated, though not fully, into nouns and verbs. When they are written they are referred to as Bijaksara, the visible form of a deity. In general all bija of deities end with the Anusvara (M) or Visarga (H).

A bija is a basic mantra, usually of one syllable, which is understood to be the audible form of a deity. OM being the Supreme Bija and Mantra. Generally, bija-mantra consists of a single letter "A" but sometimes it constitutes several syllables "AUM". Some bija-mantras are made up of compound letters, such as the mantra HREEM. There are words that do not quite fit the definition of a seed syllable called Samput, but which function in more or less the same way. SVAHA – comes from Vedic ritual and is used at the end of Buddhist mantras. PHAT – a very ancient Indian magical word. Their meaning is subtle and mystical.

The form of the bija-mantra is the form of the deity signified by it. There are four great Goddess bija-mantras that govern the prime forms of energy as magnetic force, electrical force, heat, and delight. This is a Tantric teaching that reflects the Vedic Word and the four main Vedic deities.

HRIM (pronounced as Hreem) is the primary mantra of the Great Goddess, and awakens the soul to the force of divine love and truth. KRIM (pronounced Kreem) is the great mantra of Kali, the Goddess of energy and transformation. HUM (pronounced Hoom) is a Shiva mantra but also a mantra of Chandi, the fierce form of Kali. It is used to destroy negativity and creates great passion and vitality. SHRIM (pronounced Shreem) is a mantra of love, devotion and beauty, relating to Lakshmi, the Goddess of Beauty and divine grace. The bija of the five elements are, HAM – ether, YAM – air. RAM – fire, VAM – water, LAM – earth.

Written in the proper way with the proper spirit, the concentrated power of bija is capable of manifesting the latent Devas or Buddhas within the practitioner. Without proper knowledge, the letters are nothing more than profane markings. It is said that those who have mastered bija may disperse with all texts, mantras or images, as they can see the world of Buddha in a single letter.

Bija can be written in any Brahmic script but they are generally written in Devanagari by Hindu's, and Siddhamatrka, Ranjana and Uchen by Mahayana and Vjayrana Buddhists. As well as being spoken, bija can be written on the body or in mandalas and yantras using a pen, brush or coloured sand.

A as OM

As mystical Buddhism established itself outside of India with non-sanskrit speaking peoples, the complex philosophies of Hindu Tantra and the esoteric significance of the Sanskrit alphabet were incorporated into Tantric Buddhism with several changes. The letters were perceived as 'exploding' from the emptiness or Sanyota, rather than originating from Sabda Brahman, meaning the letters were 'uncreated' existing according to natural principles and learned through insight. Strict adherence to classical Sanskrit pronunciation of mantras was disregarded as Buddhism spread outside of India. The letter A replaced Om as the Seed Syllable Supreme. It is the seed syllable of Mahavainocana, the Great Buddha of Light, and meditation on this letter became an important esoteric practise.

Heart Sutra Bija

The Heart Sutra is one of the most famous Buddhist Sutras, with a mantra that can be condensed into a single syllable – the bija Dhih. Dhi is the Vedic root of 'Dhih' which incorporates a range of meanings including: to perceive, to think, to reflect, understanding, intelligence, knowledge and wisdom. Dhrih is sometimes combined with 'mma' resulting in the complex syllable 'Dhrihmma' associated with the Heart Sutra.

HUM (Hoom)

HUM is frequently the last syllable of a mantra. The diagram of HUM shows how it is put together in a single stack from various elements which are more or less the same in all Brahmic scripts. Hum with the long vowel 'u' is called the Kurcha Bija and is the mantra of the Mother worshipped by heroes (viras). The Bhutadamara also describes it as the mantra of Mahakala.

ह्लि
Hri
Bija - seed syllable

ह्लीं ह्लिः
Hrim Hrih
Bija Mantra

स्वाहा फट्
Svaha Phat
Bija words

ह्लीं क्रीं श्रीं हूं
Hrim Krim Shrim Hum
4 Great Goddess Bija Mantras

हं यं रं वं लं
HAM YAM RAM VAM LAM
ether air fire water earth
Bija of the five elements

औं
Devanagari

अं
Siddham

AMH - the seed syllable supreme
A as OM

Ranjana

Uchen

वि
Dhi
bija

विः
Dhih
bija mantra

Dhihmma
complex syllable

Heart Sutra Bija

M

H

U
long vowel

ether
wind
fire
water
earth

the architecture of HUM (hoom)

Chakra Bija

In Hindu mythology, Brahma the Creator first showed himself as a golden embryo of sound. He was a vowel, vibrating outward, the sound echoed back upon itself and became water and wind. In Tantra, this power is called Matrika Shakti, the inherent feminine creative energy behind the letters that make up words. It is said that each letter of the Sanskrit alphabet has a corresponding sound vibration both in the subtle energy channels of our bodies and in the cosmos. When these sound vibrations resonate with a corresponding vibration within us they create thoughts, then these thoughts gradually manifest the grosser forms of feelings and then speech. The Matrika Shakti resides in our energy body and rises of its own volition into consciousness, manifesting as our thoughts.

Mantras sounded in the Sanskrit language are designed to create sounds that literally vibrates the body. In Vedic healing, specific mono-syllable seed sounds or bija-mantra were developed to create balance and harmony in the human body, mind and soul. Each and every part of our body functions at a specific rhythm and pulse, and when our systems are balanced and tuned with each other, we experience perfect harmony and health. An imbalance in our bodies could lead to mental, physical or emotional disease.

The sounds and syllables emitting from the different parts of the body are shown in diagrammatic presentations. In the Tantric ritual of Matrika Nyasa, the matrikas (letters) are assigned to positions of the human body, the practitioner touches the appropriate area as he recites the alphabet. In Kundalini Yoga, certain letters are grouped together with each one of the Chakras, the 7 centers of transformation, of psychic or mental energy into spiritual energy, of the human body.

Kundalini

Kundalini is the form of the Goddess resting in Muladhara as a coiled serpent. As long as this energy remains dormant the student will engage in an outward, sensuous life, and live an ordinary life like any unconscious animal. When Kundalini is activated it turns inward and the student takes to a spiritual path.

When creation takes place, it is said that reversed coition of Shiva/Shakti takes place, and Bindhu or seed is deposited in Prakriti, resulting in the birth of the Kundalini Goddess in the nature and form of letters. Kundalini is represented as a coiled serpent with 51 coils, which are the subtle forms of the sounds of Vedic Sanskrit. This sound evolves from Para state at Mulhadra to Vaikori state in the Vissaudhra chakra, the throat center where articulate speech comes from. One coil is bindhu, two coils is Prakriti-Pirusa, three coils are three shaktis, Iccha, Jnana and Kriyan and the three gunas, sattvas, rajas and tamas, representing will, knowledge and action.

The coiled energy of the serpent Goddess Kundalini when activated, rises from the base of the spine to the point just above the head, through ritual use of the chakra energy system. The practise of performing this ritual is called Kundalini yoga, just one of the many forms of yoga, all derived from the same source. Most forms of yoga use mediation and chanting of bija-mantra to expand ones consciousness and help in healing the mind, body and spirit.

Chakra

Emerging sometime between 1150 and 500 BCE, the concept of a chakra system features in the tantric and yogic traditions of Hinduism and Buddhism. The ancient spiritual Indian texts refer to various systems with variations in the number of chakras and their location. The most commonly known is the more recent system with seven main chakras, dating to around the eighth century CE.

The Sanskrit word 'chakra' translates into 'wheel' which can be thought of as a vortex that both receive & radiate energy. They are the 7 major energy centers in the human body, that run from the base of the spine to the crown of the head. Emotions, physical health, & mental clarity affect how well each chakra can filter energy. This in turn dictates how pure the energy is that's emitted from the body. Chakras are not materially real, they are to be understood as situated, not in the gross body, but in the subtle or etheric body. Repositories of psychic energies, they govern the whole condition of being.

Chakras are usually represented as lotuses. Each of the 50 petals of the first 6 chakras are associated with one of the letter of the Sanskrit alphabet. At the center of each chakra is a bija-mantra, the symbolic representation of the energy pattern of each chakra, its essence. When performing these mantras, the individual resonates with the particular chakra. Each chakra is characterized by a category of sounds, by a special colour of inner light and by special forms of transcendental awareness.

Chakra Bija

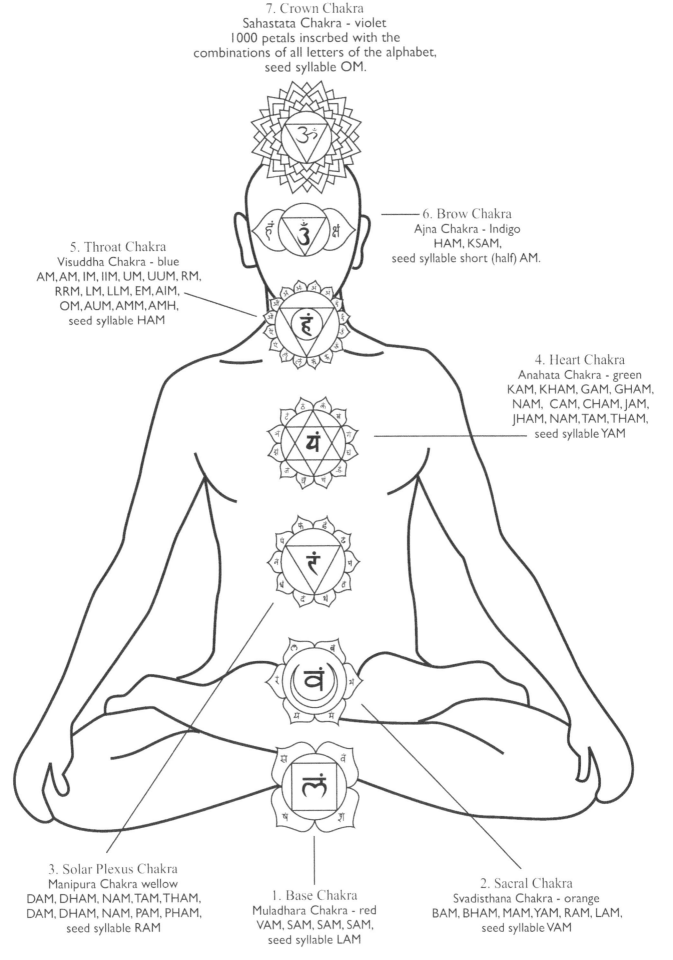

7. Crown Chakra
Sahastata Chakra - violet
1000 petals inscrbed with the
combinations of all letters of the alphabet,
seed syllable OM.

6. Brow Chakra
Ajna Chakra - Indigo
HAM, KSAM,
seed syllable short (half) AM.

5. Throat Chakra
Visuddha Chakra - blue
AM, AM, IM, IIM, UM, UUM, RM,
RRM, LM, LLM, EM, AIM,
OM, AUM, AMM, AMH,
seed syllable HAM

4. Heart Chakra
Anahata Chakra - green
KAM, KHAM, GAM, GHAM,
NAM, CAM, CHAM, JAM,
JHAM, NAM, TAM, THAM,
seed syllable YAM

3. Solar Plexus Chakra
Manipura Chakra wellow
DAM, DHAM, NAM, TAM, THAM,
DAM, DHAM, NAM, PAM, PHAM,
seed syllable RAM

1. Base Chakra
Muladhara Chakra - red
VAM, SAM, SAM, SAM,
seed syllable LAM

2. Sacral Chakra
Svadisthana Chakra - orange
BAM, BHAM, MAM, YAM, RAM, LAM,
seed syllable VAM

Mantra

Mantra is an organic language in which sound and meaning correspond as sound-ideas. The spiritual expression of sound is found in poetry and music, which are synthesized in the one profound and all embracing vibration of the sacred syllable or bija-mantra. In Tantra, everything in Creation is formed from air that resonates as sound. This sound is called the "Word". This is not ordinary words or Sabda of which speech is composed, it is mantra or "instruments of thought" which create a mental picture with its sound.

In India, not only the Word but every sound of which it consists, every letter of the alphabet, is looked upon as a sacred symbol. The letters of the alphabet are mantras or sacred prayer syllables, linking the practitioner to a particular divine principle. Each letter is charged with energy that creates vibrations in the inner consciousness of the devotee. Mantra are tools for thinking and worshipping. Meditating on mantra, shapes the mind and makes it pure.

Mantra is a sacred utterance, a magical sound. A syllable, word or group of words spoken or written in Sanskrit, believed to have psychological and spiritual powers. The earliest were composed in Vedic Sanskrit in India and are at least 3000 years old. They are now found in various schools of Hinduism, Jainism, Budhism, Sikhism and their equivalent can be found in Zoroastrianism, Taoism, Christianity and elsewhere.

Mantras are masculine (solar), feminine (lunar) or neuter. A female mantra is called a Vidya, meaning knowledge. Solar and neuter forms are called mantras. A mantra can only work if it is received from a guru who has received it in an unbroken line from its first Rishi. Only then do they have life, according to the tradition. There are however, exceptions to this, some Tantras prescribe methods of purification for mantras received in dreams. In general, mantras are usually written from left to right using the Devanagari, Siddhamatrika, Ranjana and Uchen scripts. But they can be written in any of the Brahmi derived scripts of Asia.

Bija-Mantra

Bija-mantra reflect the archetypical vibration behind all phenomenal objects, the vibration of the Divine Word itself. This is not a religious belief but the vibrational energy of cosmic intelligence that forms all things. The most effective mantras are the seed syllables or bija, single or combinations of sounds containing the sum total of the divinity. The greatest of all these is Om, the Pranava Mantra, the source of all bija and mantra, the mother of all sounds. Om is the manifestation of Bindhu, the creative impulse of the cosmos. Composed of the elements A U M – signifying the Trimurti, the creation, preservation and dissolution of the world.

Bija, like mantra are spoken with the mind and heard by the heart. Bija-mantra do not have to have any literal meaning, they are mystical words, they can be spoken, sung and chanted individually or strung together to from mantras. In Vedic terms, the bija-mantra SHRIM is a Soma mantra. It gives love, joy, bliss, beauty and delight. It has the light of the moon and governs the mind and the realm between the atmosphere and heaven. It purifies and integrates the various aspects of our nature and renders them into ambrosia.

Written Mantra

Written mantras add to the spiritual power of the spoken mantra. The Avira mantra "Om All Pervading, Imperishable One" is the mantra of the Great Buddha called Damichi in Japan and Mahaircana in Tibet. Written in Siddhamatrika, the mantra is arranged in the form of a Stupa or temple and read from the bottom upwards.

Om Mani Padme Hum is probably the most famous Tantric mantra, particularity associated with Tibetan Buddhism. The mantra of the Boddhisattva called Avalokkitesvara, the Mahavaircana, the compassionate aspect of Buddha. It is written from right to left in any of four scripts styles.

The Kalachalra mantra can be condensed into a complex syllable called The Powerful Ten. It is formed of seven syllables, Om, Ha, Ksa, Ma, La, Va, Ra, Tam, plus the visarga, bindhu and nada to make ten. It is formed using a technique called Kutaksara or "heap syllables" in which seven syllables have been arranged on top of each other to create a mystical monogram or magic sigil. It has been written in both Siddhamatrika and Ranjana scripts.

Bija and mantra such as Hum and Om Mani Padme Hum are written in a circle arrangements referred to as Mantra Chakras (thought wheel) can be composed of one letter bija-mantra forms or from the bija of one or more deities, especially Boddhisattavas.

हूं हां हीं हूं हैं हौं हः

hum   hram   hreem   hraim   hroom   hroum   hrahada

Bija mantra - Devanagari

ॐ भगवत्यै विद्‌महे माहेश्वर्यै च धीमहि । तन्नो अन्नपूर्णा प्रचोदयात् ॥

Om We know the Supreme Goddess, contemplate the Great Supreme Divinity. May Annapurna grant us increase.

Maja mantra - Devanagari

Dainichi Mantra - Siddham

Honourific Uchen

Ume (cursive ornamental)

Lantsa (Ranjana)

Vartu (cursive Ranjana)

OM MANI PADME HUM (Tibetan)
written mantra

Kalachakra - Siddham

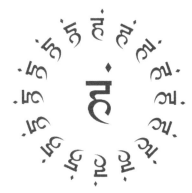

Hum - Devanagari

Bodhisattvas - Lantsa
mantra chakra

Om Mani Padme Hum - Uchen

Yantra

Meaning 'instrument' in Sanskrit, a yantra is a geometrical diagram which can represent a deity or divine figure, making the process of evolution conscious to the adept of Tantra. Yantras are meant to inspire inner visualization and experience in the worshipper. All primal shades of a yantra are psychological symbols corresponding to inner states of human consciousness. The sacred symbols of the process of involution and evolution.

Generally made of several concentric figures (squares, circles, lotuses, triangles, point). The point (bindu) at the center of the yantra signifies unity, the origin, the principle of manifestation and emanation. When these concentric figures are gradually growing away from its center (bindu) in stages, this is a symbol of the process of macrocosmic evolution. When they are gradually growing towards its center, this is a symbol of the process of microcosmic evolution.

The Sanskrit syllables inscribed on yantras are essentially 'thought forms' representing divinities or cosmic powers, which exert their influence by means of sound-vibration. In the Dharmic traditions, all phenomena are essentially the 'formation of vibration and resonance'. All form arises from the bija-mantra OM.

Bija and mantra are frequently substituted for anthropomorphic images on yantra because their concentrated natures makes them more potent than coarse images. Commonly the letters of the alphabet are placed on the outer rim or edge of the yantra and the mantra and bija within. Recitation of those divine powers inherent in the letters is sound to anchor the meditator in the world of the Supreme.

Sri Yantra

Cymatics is the study of the inter relationship of sound and form, and the study of cymatics has proven that the visual form of Om is the Sri Yantra, the Divine Plan. Hans Jenny discovered that when Om is spoken (aum), the pattern of circles and triangles of the Sri Yantra appears in sand on a resonator plate, or in an electron vibration field sensor called a Tonoscope. Jenny also discovered that when the sounds of the Vedic alphabet are spoken, the written form of the letter appears. The sound of the letter is the vibratory form of that letter. Images of the Sri Yantra have always shown the 51 sounds of Vedic Sanskrit are distributed throughout the diagram of the Sri Yantra.

Matrika Yantra

The Matrika Yantra is the divine plan (Sri Yantra) of the Universe expressed in words and syllables of the 51 letters of Vedic Sanskrit, accompanied in the rays of the light as Kala (sun), they sustain the Universe. The vowels are 16 aspects (15 of night and one transcendent) of Soma (moon). The remaining consonants from ka to bha are the 24 aspects of the sun, and the consonants from ma to the last are ten aspects of fire (agni).

The Matrika Yantra is to be drawn with saffron (kesara) for Shakti worship and with ashes (bhasma) for Shiva worship. It contains all the 51 matrikas and is used in the first of the ten rites to purify a mantra (samskara) after it has been received from a guru. On the petals of the yantra are the consonants while the vowels are in the eight spokes. In the centre is the syllable Hsauh while in the cardinal directions is the Bam bija and in the intermediate directions the Tham bija-mantra.

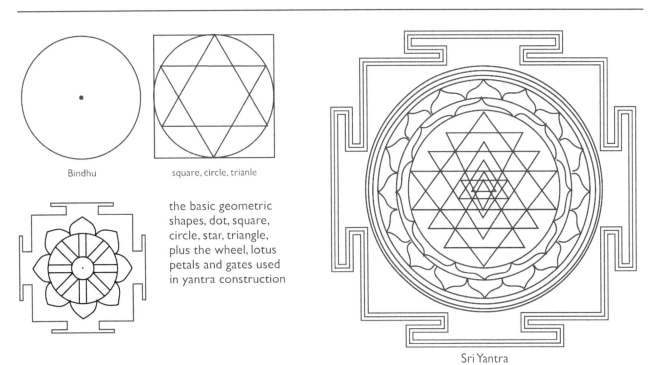

Bindhu

square, circle, trianle

the basic geometric shapes, dot, square, circle, star, triangle, plus the wheel, lotus petals and gates used in yantra construction

Sri Yantra

simple and complex yantras

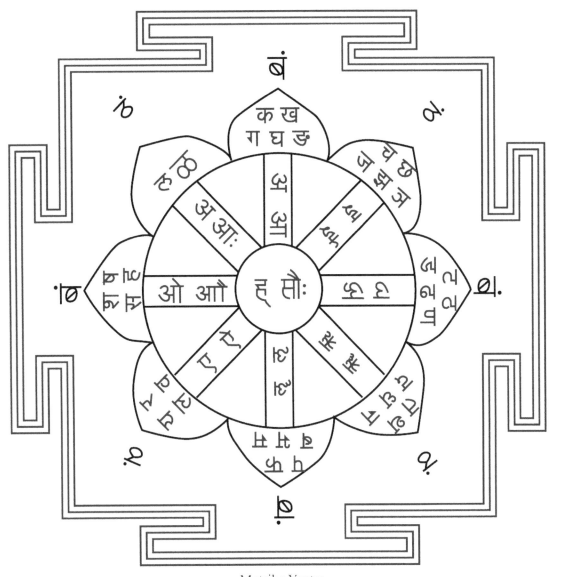

Matrika Yantra

Sak Yant

Sak Yant is a form of tattoo art that originated with the Tai tribes of southwest China and northwest Vietnam over 2,000 years ago. Sak means 'tattoo' and Yant means 'yantra', in the Thai language. A form of mystical diagram used in Dharmic religion, they are considered to be sacred designs that offer power, protection, charisma and other benefits to the wearer. While the tradition of tattooing itself originated with indigenous tribal animism, it became closely tied with the Hindu-Buddhist concept of yantra or mystical geometric patterns used in meditation. The designs consist of several graphic elements including pictorial and abstract renderings of Buddha and other deities, sacred animals called Himapant, and Pali phrases written in various sacred scripts.

Himapant animals are mystical animals from the ancient mystical Indian forest of Himapant. The list of Himapant animals is endless, it includes insects, fish, birds, reptiles, mammals and hybrids like mermaids, dragons, griffins and demigods, representing elemental powers and Bodhisattvas.

The scripts used for yant designs varies culturally and geographically. In Thailand and Cambodia, both the Old Khmer and its modern variant are used (Khom Tai). In Thailand, the Old Khmer script is considered to be an especially powerful magic script. In northern Thailand and Myanmar, the Lanna, Shan or Tai Lue variant scripts are employed in yant design. In Laos they use the Lao Thai script. These scripts are used to spell out abbreviated syllables from Pali incantations.

In the 21st century, Sak Yant is mainly practised in Thailand and to a lesser extent in Cambodia, Laos and Myanmar. Their popularity among the masses, fueled by western celebrity endorsement, have turned many modern day Thais to view Sak Yant as nothing more than stylish amulets and talismans or good luck charms, so much so that some are asking for a complete ban of any tattoo of religious figures like Buddha.

Yant Tant Crao Paetch (Diamond Armour Yantra)

The Thai Buddhist monk called Luang Phor Porn, who was ordained in 1895, found the hidden mystery of the Yant Grao Paetch or Diamond Armour Yant/Kata. It consists of the kata called the Eight Direction Mantra. It is said that if chanted consistently and regularly without fail, it can make one immensely wealthy. Its powers are said to be an invincibility spell, as well as providing an extensive set of Buddhist blessings for luck, karma improvement, prosperity, and protection against all ailments and dangers, as well as providing a wealthy future. Along with the Gao Yord Yant, it is one of the fundamental yant designs. Without the Grao Paetch Yant, it would be impossible for many other yant to exist, due to the fact that many other yant contain the same kata inscribed in the structure.

Yant Hah Taew (Five Sacred Lines)

This yant dates back over 200 years to the ancient kingdom of Lanna in northern Thailand. The Buddhist monk, Kruba Kam designed the yant around 1296, the same time as the city of Chiang Mai was founded. A series of five magic spells or katas written in Old Khmer script, the original lines have been completely replaced over the centuries. They are chanted 108 times before entering a higher state of meditation.

Yant Jin Jok Sawng (Two Tailed Gecko Yantra)

A Himapant yantra, the two tailed gecko is inscribed with a kata or mantra down the middle of its back. Considered lucky, it is used by shopkeepers for business and general finances and gamblers. It is often made with metal or on cloth.

Yant Gao Yord

Also called Yant Kru or Master Yant, the Gao Yord is a most sacred Buddhist yant with very wide ranging powers of protection. It is quite possibly the most important of all available yant designs, because of its universal power. It is the first yant design given to a follower of a yant master, tattooed before other personal designs are added to the body. There are three main variations of the basic design, which represents the nine peaks of mount Meru, the abode of Lord Brahma and other deities in Hindu mythology. In Buddhist mythology, the mountain is known as Sumeru.

The spiral designs are called Unnalome, indicating the earthly distractions we encounter in our daily lives. As we grow older and wiser this spiral gradually decreases until it becomes a straight line pointing upwards. This signifies the path to Nirvana or true enlightenment. The set of three ovals called Ong Pra (Buddha's body) are a representation of the Lord Buddha and this grouping of three ovals can be seen in many other yant designs. The Gao Yord Yant has nine Buddhas each bestowing special powers or spells.

In some versions of the yant, there is a mantra/kata, Buddhist Psalm or incantation written at the base of the design, in various scripts, Khmer, Shan, Lanna, and gives the abbreviations for the names of these Buddhas – a, song, wi, su, loe, pu, sa, pu, pa. It does not say anything as it is a chant, it is not a phrase as such but rather the use of syllables to represent certain elements involved with Buddhist magic.

Other versions of the yant design feature a central patchwork of small squares, a magic box, although the lines are not shown in some designs. Each square contains an abbreviation, written in Old Khmer, for the names of the protection spells the yant will bestow. The number of small squares varies according to the design.

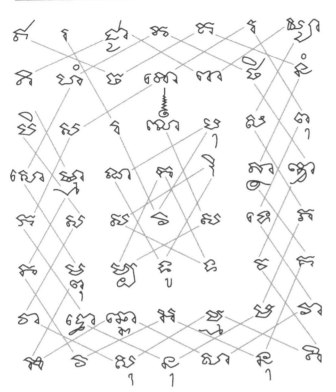

Yant Grao Paetch / Diamond Amour

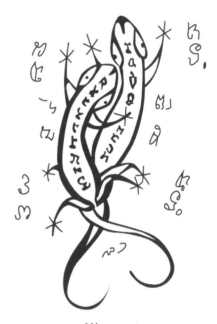

Yant Hah Taew / five sacred lines

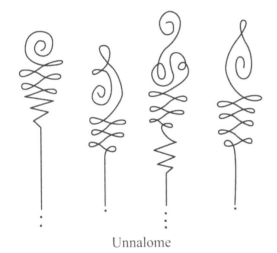

Unnalome

Himapant
Yant Jim Jok Sawng Haeng / 2 tailed gecko

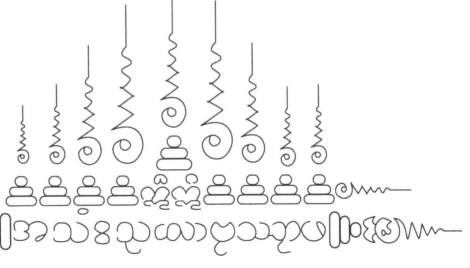

Yant Gao Yord

Mandalas

Mandala meaning 'circle' in Sanskrit, is a sacred, symbolic diagram, a visual aid to attain desirable mental states. A mandala can be defined in two ways, as a schematic representation of the universe or, internally as a guide for several psychological practises that take place in many Asian traditions, including meditation.

A traditional mandala is a simple or complex blueprint of a 'temple of the Gods', as well as the entire universe. It is an integral part of Hindu and Buddhist tradition. They are not to be confused with yantra, which are mainly geometric. Simplistically speaking, mandalas are used by Buddhists and yantras are used by Hindu's.

Hindu mandalas are also superficially similar to Rangoli, pretty, traditional, freestyle designs that differ stylistically across India. Celebrated in local festivals, Rangoli are mainly drawn and coloured using dyed rice flour, also sand, brick dust and flower petals.

In Tantric Buddhism, there are four types of mandala. The Maha Mandalas depict the Buddhas and Bodhisattvas in human form. Somaya Mandalas show them as objects. Dharma Mandalas show them as bija. Karma Mandalas are three dimensional sculptural mandalas like Angkor Wat.

Painting

Mandalas are objects of devotion in Hindu and Buddhist tantra and they are also used in Jainism. They can be painted on paper, wood, stone, cloth or even on a wall. They are painstakingly created with coloured sand, entirely by hand. From tracing the outline design to filling the sand, grain by grain, they can take weeks to build. This labour intensive method is both an artistic and spiritual practise, and once the mandala is complete it is followed by its ceremonial destruction. It is swept away into a jar and emptied into a nearby body of water as a blessing. The act of destruction is there to remind us of the impermanence of life. A powerful metaphor for the creative process.

In temples and monasteries, monks are taught the three lessons of mandala creation, maintaining discipline, perseverance and letting go. In the beginning, monks are not allowed to use coloured sand, working only with white sand to perfect and hone their skills. Any mistakes and the mandala is wiped away and begun again. When the process of maintaining discipline has manifested, the next lesson begins.

Perseverance is essential to the completion of any creative endeavor, thing will not always run smoothly. Ego, creative block, forgetfulness, veto of ideas and sabotage, along with a host of other gremlins, will obstruct the completion of a project. Only when the task is complete can the monk move on the final lesson of letting go. Everything is in the past, let go and focus on the next task in hand. This is the way in which monks are taught to maintain creative flexibility and enjoy the work involved in the creative process.

Symbology

Some mandalas are associated with a symbolic palace. In the center of the mandala lies the palace, which has four gates associated to the four quarters of the world and is located within several layers of circles that form a protective barrier around it. Each layer embodies a quality, eg. purity, devotion, etc. that one must obtain before accessing the palace.

Depending upon the tradition it belongs to, inside the palace, the mandala has symbols associated with different deities or cultural symbols such as the male thunderbolt symbol, or the female bell symbol, a wheel, the symbol of the Buddhist Eightfold Path, or a diamond, a symbol of a clear mind, amongst others.

On other occasions, mandalas can represent a particular deity or group of deities, which could number a few or thousands. In these cases, the deity or main deity is placed at the center of the mandala, while other deities are placed around the central image. The main deity is considered the generative force of the mandala and the secondary deities are seen as manifestations of the power of the core image.

In many traditions in which mandalas are used, the practitioner, at least metaphorically, establishes a dialogue with the symbol or deity at the core of the mandala by moving progressively from the outside toward the center. Once within the center, the practitioner is able to perceive all manifestations as part of a single underlying whole and gets closer to the goal of enlightenment or perfect understanding.

Dharma Mandalas

Dharma mandalas with only bija are regarded as the most sublime, the vision of one who is totally awake. Outside of India, the esoteric practises related to Sanskrit script, especially the writing and recitation of mantra, remained widespread but in general there was a simplification of the incredibly complex Indian tantric doctrines in China and Japan. Emphasis was placed on seed syllables especially in conjunction with mandalas.

In China, the sound mattered less than its written form. In fact, nothing in China had any real value unless put in writing. Chinese and Japanese Buddhist monks created large, complex mandalas that viewed the cosmos in the form of Buddhas represented as bijaksara.

Mandalas

geometric   pictorial   spoked   graphic

Hindu

Maha Mandala   Somaya Mandala   Dharma Mandala

Buddhist

Great Protective Circle
Radiates the mandala's
infinate colourful light

Buddha of Compassion
Represented by lotus flowers

Gate with 11 levels
Represents
the states leading to
enlightenment

64 Lotus
Petals
Represents
the purified
state of
mind

Circular Beam of Vajras
Represents industructibility

Cresent
Moon and
Half-Vajra
Symbolises
the Buddha's
body, speech
and mind

Precious Umbrella
Provides protection
from suffering

Entrance
Indicates entrance to the
mandala's eastern quadrant

anatomy of a Tantric Buddhist Karma mandala

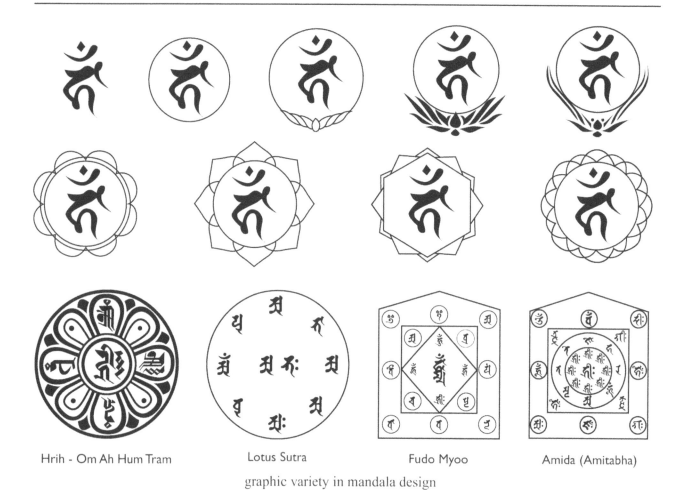

Hrih - Om Ah Hum Tram   Lotus Sutra   Fudo Myoo   Amida (Amitabha)

graphic variety in mandala design

Amitabha (Amida)

Five Buddhas of the Vajradhatu

dharma mandalas

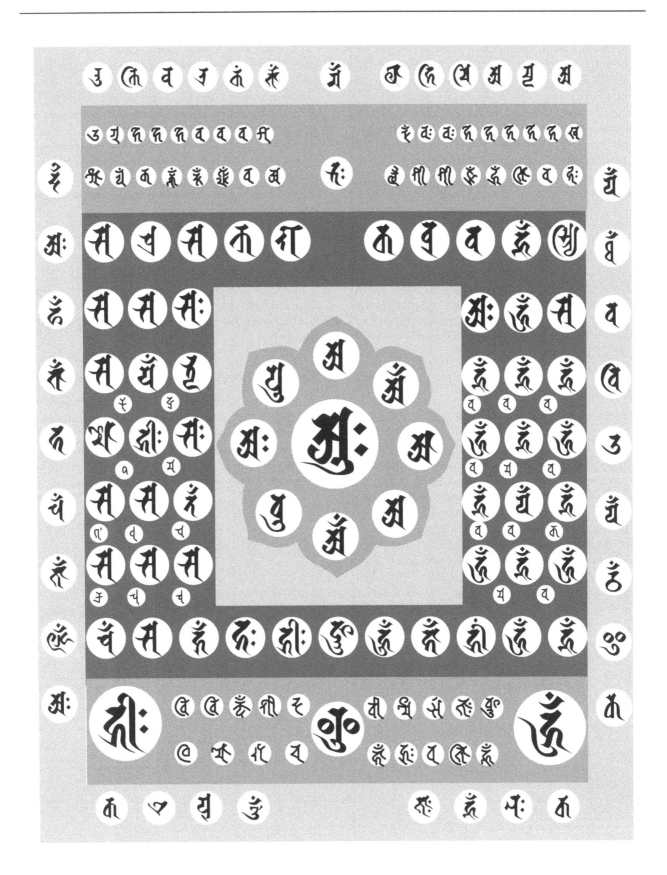

Shinji or Seed Syllable Mandala
deities symbolized by their individual bija
(copy of center panel)

Bodhisattvas

In Buddhism, Bodhisattva is a Sanskrit term for anyone who, motivated by great compassion, has generated Bodhicitta, which is a spontaneous wish and a compassionate mind to attain Buddhahood for the benefit of all sentient beings. In early Buddhism, the term Boddhisattva was primarily used to refer to specifically to Gautama Buddha in his former life. It comes from the Jakata tales, in which bodhisattva originally referred to the pre-enlightened practitioner of austerities.

Mahayana Buddhism is primarily based on the path of a bodhisattva, in which, life in this world is compared to people living in a house that is on fire. People take the world as reality, pursuing worldly projects and pleasures without realizing that the house is ablaze, due to the inevitability of death. A bodhisattva is someone who is determined to free sentient beings from Samsara and its life cycle of death, rebirth and suffering. Bodhisattvas take the bodhisattva vows in order to progress on the spiritual path towards Buddhahood. This type of mind is known as the 'mind of awakening' (bodhisattva).

Taizokai/Garbhadharu

As mystical Buddhism established itself outside of India with non-sanskrit speaking peoples, the complex philosophies of Hindu Tantra and the esoteric significance of the Sanskrit alphabet were incorporated into Mahayana and Vjrayana Buddhism, specifically China, Japan and Tibet, with several changes. One of these changes was that Buddhas and Bodhisattvas replaced the Deva and Devi of the Hindu pantheon, although the seed syllables of the Buddhas were formed in patterns similar to that of the Devas e.g. HRIM the seed syllable of Amitabha Buddha consists of H – karma, R – passion, I – calamity, M – removed, epitomizing Buddhas vow to free his followers from all evils.

In Tantra each Bodhisattvas is associated with a seed syllable. From emptiness comes the seed. From the seed, the concept of an icon develops, and from that conception, the external representation of the icon is derived. Awareness of emptiness is transformed into a seed, the seed develops into a Buddha, which may then be portrayed as an image. Written in the proper way with the proper spirit, the concentrated power of the seed syllable is capable of manifesting the latent Buddha within us. Without such proper knowledge, the letters are nothing more than profane markings.

The 13 Buddhas are often grouped together. The list is comprised of the 13 Buddhas and Bodhisattvas who are venerated on special days following a believers death. A different deity is honoured on the 7th, 27th, 37th, 47th, 57th, 67th, 77th and 100 days and on the 1st, 3rd, 7th, 13th and 33rd year anniversaries. Although they are linked in a sequence they also stand alone and can be written separately.

Sanzon (the three honoured ones)

A Buddha or Bodhisattva is often shown together with two attendants. The attendants compliment the principle symbolized in the central figure. For example, Amida attendants are Seishi or strength, and Kannon or skillful means, they are the two vehicles that bring their masters unlimited compassion to sentient beings.

Bodhisattvas

12. Mahavairocana Tathagata
Dainichi Nyorai

AMIDA
hrih

SEISHI
sah

KANNON
sa

Amida Sanzon

7. Bhaisajya Tathagata
kushi Nyorai

1. Acala Vidyaraja
Fudo Myoo

8. Avalokitesvara Bodhisattva
Kanzeon Bosatsu

2. Sakyamuni Tathagata
Shaka Nyorai

9. Sthamaprapta Bodhisattva
Seishi Bosatsu

3. Manjusri Bodhisattva
Monju Bosatsu

10. Amitabha Tathagata
Amida Nyorai

4. Samantabhadra Bodhisattva
Fugen Bosatsu

11. Aksobhya Tathagata
Ashuku Nyorai

5. Ksitigarbha Bodhisattva
Jizo Bosatsu

13. Akasagarbha Bohisattva
Kokuzo Boastsu

6. Maitreya Bodhisattva
Miroku Bosatsu

Taizokai / Garbhadhatu - The Thirteen Buddha's and Bodhisattva's

Further Reading

Print

The Blackwell Encyclopedia of Writing
Blackwell Publishing
Florian Coulmass

Sacred Calligraphy of the East
Shambala
John Stevens

The Rough Guide History of India
Rough Guides
Dilip Hiro

Digital

YOU TUBE
sanskrit
varna shishka

WEB
wikkipedia.org
ancientscripts.com
omniglot.com
script souces.org
britannica.com
hindidevanagari.com
hindupedia.com
banglapedia.com
tamilheritage.org
indianetzone.com
hinduwebsite.com
ciillibrary.org
exoticindianart.com
ancientindianwisdom,com
bhagavaditavsa.com/sound.htm
ravikhanna.com
collectivepsyche.com/cymatics
inannareturns,com/articles/shivasutras/sutra002-7.htm
visablemantra.org
tantra-kundalini.com
yogamag.net
chetanananda.com
beyondweird.com/ck/index.htm (chakras)
lantsha-vartu.org
kalachakra.org
soravj.com/showcase/yantra/yantra.htm
aghori.com/yantra

PDF
yungdrung.org/doc/Compliation_History_Zhang_Zhung.pdf
mustafasaitee.com/thesis.pdf (Devanagari typography)